CENTURY OF GENIUS: EUROPEAN THOUGHT 1600-1700

Edited by

Richard T. Vann

PRENTICE-HALL, INC.
Englewood Cliffs, New Jersey

Current printing (last number):

10   9   8   7   6   5   4   3   2   1

FOREWORD

The writings on politics—politics in no narrow sense of what goes on in those familiar smoke-filled rooms of politician's caucusing, but politics in the old Greek sense of concern for all public matters—these writings form the basis of the great eighteenth-century documents we all know, or should know, so well. For it was in the seventeenth century of Hobbes and the other writers of that "century of genius" that the realistic study of politics, perhaps never wholly absent from political writings in the Western world, reached a "take-off point" which made possible in the next century the widespread circulation of the ideas embodied in the American Declaration of Independence, the French Declaration of the Rights of Man and the Citizen, the Bills of Rights of many state constitutions and of the Federal Constitution. It is not that the seventeenth century was, except for a few Englishmen of the Puritan Revolution, democratic. Indeed Hobbes himself was by no means a democrat. It is rather that out of this matrix of ideas about man's fate here on earth, so well presented by Professor Vann in this book, there came emancipation from earlier ideas of a relatively static and ordered society in which laws were found, not made, not invented, not "passed" as statutes and bills. Without this emancipation the dynamic modern world could not have developed as it did. Professor Vann has wisely limited himself to relatively long excerpts from major thinkers, avoiding the trap of covering too many with too little for each. The student will find in this book an admirable introduction to many problems that still face the responsible citizen today.

Crane Brinton
Professor of History
Harvard University

PREFACE

The difficulties of selecting amidst the riches of seventeenth-century thought may be suggested by the fact that I have not been able to include anything by Shakespeare, Cervantes, Molière, Spinoza, or Leibniz—all men of some reputation in their national literatures. I have emphasized science and social and political thought at the expense of imaginative literature, and have tried to include what I think the generally-educated "common reader" of the time would have found most interesting (thus subordinating the more technical questions of science and philosophy to questions of method which had a more general application).

The greatest minds and the most important texts cannot be predigested into snippets. Naturally it is best to encounter them at full stretch, in their own languages. At least we must read excerpts substantial enough to show something of the range and temper of their thought. I have therefore devoted full chapters to Descartes, Hobbes, Locke, and Pascal. In addition I have given briefer extracts from a variety of sources to show the milieu in which the triumphs of seventeenth-century thought were achieved.

Except where otherwise indicated, I have made the translations. Some (of Fontenelle, Galileo, and Grotius) are adaptations of seventeenth-century translations, which I generally consulted (where available) to catch some of the turns of phrase peculiar to the period. I have generally modernized punctuation and spelling to conform to present American usage.

I wish to thank the following publishers for permission to reprint copyrighted works: Cambridge University Press, for the selection from the *Lords' Journals* (pages 5-6), from *The Eighteenth-Century Constitution,* compiled and introduced by E. N. Williams (1960) and for the selections from *Locke's Two Treatises of Government,* ed. Peter Laslett (1963) which appear on pages 121-144; Doubleday & Company, for the selections from *Discoveries and Opinions of Galileo,* translated with an introduction and notes by Stillman

Drake (© Stillman Drake, 1957) which appear on pp. 15-16, 17, 26-27, and 31-32; and Wesleyan University Press for the selection from *History and Theory*, Beiheft 4 (pages 35-37) (© Wesleyan University, 1964).

R.T.V.

CONTENTS

VII. THE RIGHTS OF MAN AND OF MERCHANT

VIII. DEFENDERS OF THE FAITH

Part I

THE MEDIUM
AND THE MESSAGE

The Book Trade and the Press

During the seventeenth century the printed word first assumed the importance which it is only now beginning to lose. The number of different titles published was greater than in the previous century and a half; more importantly, newspapers and periodicals made their appearance for the first time—not to mention a torrent of pamphlets on all subjects, especially religion and politics.

Much of the journalism of the day was ephemeral, but the magazines at least professed a loftier and less transitory purpose. The first of our learned journals, the *Journal des Sçavans* and the *Philosophical Transactions,* were both started in 1665. The latter was founded, as its editor announced in the first number, to bring to the curious researchers into the natural sciences in England the news of the pending as well as the successful experiments being carried out all over Europe—"to the end that desires after solid and useful knowledge may be further entertained, ingenious endeavors and undertakings cherished, and those addicted to and conversant in such matters may contribute what they can to the grand design of improving natural knowledge and perfecting all philosophical arts and sciences." The *Journal des Sçavans* was more interested in theology and the older branches of learning; consequently it was almost wholly devoted to book reviews. It continued a rather sober and intermittent career while other livelier reviews of books sprang up, especially in the Netherlands; the most famous was Pierre Bayle's *News of the Republic of Letters.* If there was a real Republic of Letters by the end of the century, it had been created largely by these very journals.

Unlike their sixteenth-century predecessors, writers were slowly being assured of money from the sale of their books, though copyright was still primitive; pirated editions, like those which provide so much employment for Shakespeare scholars, were still common. The practice of poets' selling the copyright of their works with sufficiently widespread for Boileau to condemn it in his *Art of Poetry* and for Milton to receive £10 (perhaps $300 in modern values) for *Paradise Lost*. The economic basis was slowly being laid for a true class of professional writers and journalists; such a class had begun to emerge in the Netherlands, center of the publishing industry, with Pierre Bayle as its first great figure.

As the sheer volume of books, magazines, and newspapers increased, reading came to displace listening as the primary way to receive not only information, but also inspiration and entertainment.* Plays were published as well as performed; even epic poetry, as *Paradise Lost* demonstrates, could be designed for the silent reader alone in his room. (Incidentally, the rebuilding of houses so that members of the family could have their own rooms and not have to live in the common hall is another feature of the seventeenth century.) Sermons, the primary entertainment of the age, were stored up for posterity, and even the intimate details of religious experience were published by the more enthusiastic English sects.

It had once been enough for governments to control preaching— "tuning her pulpits," as Queen Elizabeth used to call it—to prevent the spread of subversive or inconvenient opinions. The press presented a new challenge, and although almost every government claimed the right to prevent the publication of offending books and newspapers, regulation was seldom completely effective. Smuggling from the Netherlands, that plague spot of freedom, undermined the efforts of the godly magistrates of England and France. The Roman Inquisition was more effective, putting Galileo and Campanella in prison and Bruno to death, thus deterring others (like Descartes).

The legal mechanism for controlling printing was a system of licensing (in England administered through the stationers' gild). It was connected from the beginning with the monopolies enjoyed by privileged publishers. During the English Revolution the licensing laws remained on the books (though not very well enforced) and called forth the most famous political pamphlet of the times, Milton's *Areopagitica*. His eloquence produced no immediate results, but in 1694 the licensing system died a confused, ignominious,

---

* Marshall McLuhan's *Gutenberg Galaxy* (1962) is a stimulating discussion of this process.

and thoroughly parliamentary death in committee. Unfortunately for the privileged publishers, an eminent author, John Locke, was one of the men instrumental in deciding the future of licensing. His letters and the Commons' resolution on the subject (page 6) show that Milton's noble rhetoric was not the only influence at work.

Milton's Arguments for Freedom of the Press

From John Milton, *Areopagitica* (London, 1644), pp. 4, 11-12, 30-31, 34-35.

I deny not but that it is of greatest concernment in the church and commonwealth to have a vigilant eye how books demean themselves as well as men; and thereafter to confine, imprison, and do sharpest justice on them as malefactors. For books are not absolutely dead things, but do contain a potency of life in them to be as active as that soul was whose progeny they are; nay, they do preserve as in a vial the purest efficacy and extraction of that living intellect that bred them. I know they are as lively, and as vigorously productive, as those fabulous dragon's teeth; and being sown up and down, may chance to spring up armed men. And yet, on the other hand, unless wariness be used, as good almost kill a man as kill a good book: who kills a man kills a reasonable creature, God's image; but he who destroys a good book kills reason itself, kills the image of God, as it were in the eye. Many a man lives a burden to the earth; but a good book is the precious life-blood of a master spirit, embalmed and treasured up on purpose to a life beyond life.

*   *   *

"To the pure all things are pure": not only meats and drinks, but all kind of knowledge whether of good or evil; the knowledge cannot defile, nor consequently the books, if the will and conscience be not defiled. For books are as meats and viands are: some of good, some of evil substance; and yet God in that unapocryphal vision said without exception: "Rise, Peter, kill and eat," leaving the choice to each man's discretion. Wholesome meats to a vitiated stomach differ little or nothing from unwholesome; and best books to a naughty mind are not unappliable to occasions of evil. Bad meats will scarce breed good nourishment in the healthiest concoction*; but herein the difference is of bad books, that they to a discreet and judicious reader serve in many respects to discover, to confute, to forewarn, and to illustrate. . . . Good and evil we know in the field of this world grow up together almost inseparably, and the knowledge of good is so involved and interwoven with the knowledge of evil, and in so many cunning resemblances hardly to be discerned, that those confused seeds which were imposed upon Psyche as an incessant labor to cull out and sort asunder were not more intermixed. It was from out the rind of one apple tasted that the knowledge of good and evil, as two twins cleaving together, leaped forth into the world. And perhaps this is that doom which Adam fell into of knowing good and evil, that is to say, of knowing good by evil. As therefore the state of man now is, what wisdom can there be to choose, what continence to forebear, without the knowledge of evil? He that can apprehend and consider vice with all her baits and seeming pleasures, and yet abstain, and yet distinguish, and yet prefer that which is truly better, he is the true warfaring Christian. I cannot praise a fugitive and cloistered virtue, unexercised and unbreathed, that never sallies out and sees her adversary, but slinks out of the race where that immortal garland is to be run for, not without dust and heat. Assuredly we bring not innocence into the world; we bring impurity much rather: that which purifies us is trial, and trial is by what is contrary.

*   *   *

Lords and Commons of England, consider what nation it is whereof ye are, and whereof ye are the governors: a nation not slow and dull, but of a quick, ingenious, and piercing spirit, acute to invent, subtle and sinewy to discourse, not beneath the reach of any point the highest that human capacity can soar to. Therefore the studies of learning in her deepest sciences have been so ancient and so eminent among us that writers of good antiquity and ablest judgment have been persuaded that even the school of Pythagoras and the Persian wisdom took beginning from the old philosophy of this island. . . . And had it not been the obstinate perverseness of our prelates against the divine and admirable spirit of Wyclif to suppress him as a schismatic and innovator, perhaps neither the Bohemian Huss and Jerome, no, nor the name of Luther or of Calvin had been ever known: the glory of reforming all our neighbors had been completely ours. But now, as our obdurate clergy have with violence

* Digestion

demeaned the matter, we are become hitherto the latest and the backwardest scholars, of whom God offered to have made us the teachers.

Now once again by all concurrence of signs, and by the general instinct of holy and devout men as they daily and solemnly express their thoughts, God is decreeing to begin some new and great period in his Church, even to the reforming of Reformation itself. What does he then but reveal himself to his servants, and as his manner is, first to his Englishmen. . . . Behold now this vast city, a city of refuge, the mansion house of liberty, encompassed and surrounded with his protection. The shop of war has not there more anvils and hammers waking to fashion out the plates and instruments of armed justice in defense of beleaguered truth than there be pens and heads there, sitting by their studious lamps, musing, searching, revolving new notions and ideas wherewith to present, as with their homage and their fealty, the approaching Reformation; others as fast reading, trying all things, assenting to the force of reason and convincement.

*   *   *

Methinks I see in my mind a noble and puissant nation rousing herself like a strong man after sleep, and shaking her invincible locks; methinks I see her as an eagle mewing* her mighty youth, and kindling her undazzled eyes at the full midday beam; purging and unscaling her long-abused sight at the fountain itself of heavenly radiance; while the whole noise of timorous and flocking birds, with those also that love the twilight, flutter about, amazed at what she means, and in their envious gabble would prognosticate a year of sects and schisms. . . .

And now the time in special is, by privilege to write and speak what may help to the further discussing of matters in agitation. The temple of Janus with his two controversal faces might now not unsignificantly be set open. And though all the winds of doctrine were let loose to play upon the earth, so Truth be in the field, we do injuriously by licensing and prohibiting to misdoubt her strength. Let her and Falsehood grapple; who ever knew Truth put to the worse, in a free and open encounter?

* Moulting (probably in the sense of renewing)

John Locke's Opinion of Publishers

From a letter to Anthony Collins in John Locke, *Works* (London, 1801), X, 291.

Books seem to me to be pestilent things, and infect all that trade in them . . . with something very perverse and brutal. Printers, binders, sellers, and others that make a trade and gain out of them have universally so odd a turn and corruption of mind that they have a way of dealing peculiar to themselves, and not conformed to the good of society and that general fairness which cements mankind.

The House of Commons' Reasons for Not Renewing the Licensing Act (*1695*)

From *Lords' Journals,* XV, 545.

4. Because that Act prohibits any books to be imported (without special license) into any port in England (except London); by which means the whole foreign trade of books is restrained to London, unless the Lord Archbishop of Canterbury or the Lord Bishop of London shall, in interruption of their more important affairs in governing the Church, bestow their time *gratis* in looking over catalogues of books, and granting licenses; whereas the Commons think the other ports of the Kingdom have as good right as London to trade in books, as well as other merchandise.

8. Because that Act confirms all patents and books granted, and to be granted; whereby the sole printing of all or most of the classic authors are, and have been for many years past, together with a great number of the best books, and of most general use, monopolized by the Company of Stationers; and prohibits the importing of any such books from beyond the sea, whereby the scholars in this kingdom are forced, not only to buy them at the extravagant price they demand, but must be content with their ill and incorrect editions, and cannot

have the more correct copies which are published abroad, nor the useful notes of foreigners or other learned men upon them.

15. Because that Act prohibits printing and importing, not only heretical, seditious, and schismatical books, but all offensive books, and doth not determine what shall be adjudged offensive books; so that, without doubt, if the late King James had continued in the throne till this time, books against Popery would . . . have been deemed offensive books.

Language, Style, and Audience

It is sometimes suggested that the eighteenth century was an age of journalists who popularized the profound philosophy and science of the seventeenth. Such a judgment is obviously influenced by the stereotype of the "shallow Enlightenment"; furthermore, it overlooks one of the most remarkable characteristics of seventeenth-century thought: its consistent attempt to be popular.

Popularity meant, in the first place, writing in the modern languages rather than in Latin. At the beginning of the century Latin still enjoyed its immense prestige as the language which Vergil and Cicero spoke and which every learned man in Europe still understood. So shrewd an observer as Bacon was in no doubt that English, after all, would never be suitable for any really serious writing. At the end of his life he had *The Advancement of Learning* put into Latin, and even hired Hobbes to help translate his *Essays* as well. (The Italian proverb *traduttore, tradittore*—to translate is to betray—can seldom have been more appropriate; two generations later Englishmen looked back to Bacon's superb English and thought of him as the founder of English prose.) But by the end of the century, Latin was giving way everywhere—at least in Western Europe—to the vernacular. It was losing both its power to inspire creative writing (Milton is the last man to write great Latin verse) and its universality. Whereas Bacon had thought he could influence the intellectuals of the Continent only in Latin, by 1700 Vico's knowledge of Latin did not rescue him from provinciality, since, not knowing English or French, he was cut off from most of the advanced thought of his time.

As long as the best thought of Europe was expressed in Latin, it could be shared only by a minority. To some extent this minority was defined by social class; a poor country boy like Shakespeare could not enrich his style with the graces which came from a thorough knowledge of the classical languages. But the most important division was of the sexes: Latin was the language of the schools and hence of men, while the vernacular languages were—mother tongues. A profound split in the mind and emotions can be seen in an intellectual like Erasmus, a master of Latin eloquence who had only a tourist knowledge of any modern language. He seemed to have forgotten his native Dutch altogether, until his last words: "Dear God." For these that Latinity which was the glory of Europe was inadequate. There are, after all, things for which only the language of nurse, mother, home, of the body—in short, the "vulgar tongues"—will serve.

The task of most writers in the seventeenth century, then, was to bring all the subtlety and sophistication learned from Latin to enhance the force and mysterious reverberation of the mother tongue. And the audience to be appealed to was the plain man, but even more the plain woman, since the active participation of women in the intellectual life of Europe was now an accomplished fact. Often enough it was mocked; Molière's sallies are famous, and "bluestocking" is a seventeenth-century coinage. But those who came to scoff at least remained to sell, as Fontenelle confesses (page 11).

Such an audience demanded wit, courtesy, and conciseness. This was not merely a matter of literary polish; there were philosophical reasons for simple speech (page 9). The English philosophical tradition even in its beginnings was marked by an unusual sensitivity to linguistic problems, to ambiguity and what Hobbes called "insignificant discourse." Locke, though by no means free of these offenses, preached better than his practice in his *Essay Concerning Human Understanding*. Both Locke and Hobbes felt that philosophy in English—Anglo-Saxon English—might be exempt from the absurdities too easily perpetrated in Latin. Stripped of their polysyllabic trappings, the imposing fallacies of scholastic philosophy would collapse.

Science, too, could be written in the vernacular, as Descartes and especially Galileo were to prove. The latter wrote all his major works after 1610 in a pungent and witty Italian, which has earned him the reputation of being one of the greatest Italian stylists of his times. The appearance of scientific treatises in the vernacular (particularly of a dangerous tendency regarding cosmology) was scarcely more welcome to some churchmen than the vernacular theological treatises and Biblical translations of the previous century. This was certainly one reason for Galileo's ultimate imprisonment.

Descartes was also, in his later works, his own popularizer, especially in the *Discourse on Method,* which was not only written in a direct and even artless French, but even begins with directions to the reader on where to stop in case he cannot finish the sixty-page work in one sitting. But perhaps the greatest achievement was Pascal's *Provincial Letters:* theology in the vernacular again, but now brought from the study into the salon and made to speak with a moral passion sharpened by irony and wit. It was writing which showed what the French language was capable of; and not only French, for a hundred years later Gibbon referred to it as a model for *The Decline and Fall of the Roman Empire.*

So great was the power of French writers, reinforced by that of the French armies, that French seemed on the verge of assuming the mantle of Latin as the new international language. For all the monuments of Spanish, Italian, and English prose, a work could reach the greatest number of readers only in French translation. One of the ironies of history is that English thought made its first great impact upon France and the rest of the continent through the translations made by Huguenots who had taken refuge in England after the revocation of the Edict of Nantes. Men like Pierre Coste, improving their English originals with the matchless clarity of French, were in the end to repay the French monarchy for their forced acquisition of English.

Classical Languages Conduce to Absurdity

From Thomas Hobbes, *Leviathan* (London, 1651), chap. iv.

. . . If it be a false affirmation to say a quadrangle is round, the word *round quadrangle* signifies nothing, but is a mere sound. So likewise if it be false to say that virtue can be poured or blown up and down, the words *inpoured virtue, inblown virtue* are as absurd and insignificant as a *round quadrangle.* And therefore you shall hardly meet with a senseless and insignificant word that is not made up of some Latin or Greek names.

Locke Improved in Translation

From the translator's preface (by Pierre Coste) to Locke's *Essay Concerning Human Understanding* (Amsterdam, 1700).

It seems to me that a translator is rather like a minister plenipotentiary. The comparison is somewhat grandiose, and I fear lest I be criticized for making too much of a trade which is not generally very well thought of; but be that as it may, I think that neither the translator nor the plenipotentiary could operate to best advantage if their discretionary powers were too strictly curtailed. . . . Whenever I have had difficulty in understanding a passage in English because it contained some doubtful term (the English are less careful in these matters than we are) I have tried, after I have thoroughly grasped what the author was trying to say, to express the thing so clearly in French that nobody could possibly fail to understand it. It is mainly in its clarity and lucidity that French is superior to all other languages—including the classical languages, insofar as I can judge.

French to Be the Universal Language

From *News of the Republic of Letters* (Amsterdam, November 1685), article vi (by Pierre Bayle). Translated from French.

From now on the French language will be the bridge of communication for all the countries of Europe. It is a language which we might truly call transcendental, for the same reason that compels philosophers to give that title to natures which spread far and wide and force themselves into every category.

The Royal Society's Rules of Style

From Thomas Sprat, *History of the Royal Society* (London, 1667), pp. 111, 113.

. . . There is one thing more about which the Society has been most solicitous, and that is the manner of their discourse, which, unless they had been very watchful to keep in due temper, the whole spirit and vigor of their design had been soon eaten out by the luxury and redundance of speech. The ill effects of this superfluity of talking have already overwhelmed most other arts and professions, insomuch that . . . I can hardly forbear . . . concluding that eloquence ought to be banished out of all civil societies, as a thing fatal to peace and good manners. . . . They have therefore been more rigorous in putting in execution the one remedy that can be found for this extravagance; and that has been a constant resolution to reject all amplifications, digressions, and swellings of style; to return back to the primitive purity and shortness, when men delivered so many things almost in an equal number of words. They have exacted from all their members a close, naked, natural way of speaking; positive expressions, clear sense, a native easiness, bringing all things as near the mathematical plainness as they can, and preferring the language of artisans, countrymen, and merchants before that of wits or scholars.

Confessions of a Popularizer

From the Preface to Fontenelle, *History of Oracles* (Paris?, 1687). Translated from French.

Not long since there fell into my hands a small book written in Latin, *De Oraculis Ethnicorum* or *Of the Heathen Oracles,* composed by Mr. Van Dale, a Doctor of Medicine. . . . The whole work appeared to me to be full of knowledge of antiquity and profound learning, which gave me a great desire to translate it, so that the ladies and those gentlemen even who do not willingly read Latin might not be deprived of so agreeable and useful a discourse. But I reflected that a translation of this book (though excellent in the original) would not be so good if too closely turned into French; for Mr. Van Dale wrote only for the learned, and had reason to neglect those ornaments and delicacies which they do not esteem. He cites a great number of passages very faithfully and his versions are wonderfully exact when he translates from the Greek. He enters also into a discussion of many points of criticism which, though they are not always necessary, yet they are always curious; and this he does to gratify the learned, who care little for flourishing reflections, discourses of morality, or pleasant wit.

Besides this, Mr. Van Dale has no objections to very often inter-rupting the thread of his discourse and introducing other things which present themselves; and from one digression he sometimes passes to another, and perhaps to a third. And herein he is again cor-rect, since those for whom he writes are fitted for the fatigue of read-ing, and this learned disorder does not at all embarrass or perplex them. But those for whom I design this translation would have been very ill served if I had followed this method. The ladies and, quite frankly, most of the men of this country are indeed more pleased with the graces and turns of expression and thought than with the most exact enquiries and most profound arguments; and being very lazy, they desire to read books written in a facile manner, so that they may be less obliged to pay careful attention.

For this reason I gave up the idea of making a translation . . . I have changed the whole arrangement of the book and have cut out whatever appeared to me of too little profit in itself, or of too little pleasure to make amends for whatever small profit it had. I have not only added all the ornaments I could think of, but also many things which prove or elucidate what is in question. . . . In short, I have reconceived and rearranged the whole work and have put it into the same order that I would have chosen . . . had I as much knowledge as Mr. Van Dale; but since I am far from it, I have borrowed his learning and ventured to make use of my own wit and fancy, such as it is, to adorn it.

Part II
REASON, SENSE, AND SCIENCE

Introduction

At the beginning of the seventeenth century the picture of the world which most Europeans held, and had held for almost two millennia, was becoming increasingly incoherent and unsatisfying. This picture, or cosmology, had told sixty generations of men how the moral, political, and physical orders supported each other and composed an admirable harmony of the universe. It was most fully set forth in the encyclopedic works of Aristotle, which were esteemed as authoritative in physics, physiology, and literary criticism no less than in ethics and politics, and which were the basis of the higher education of the time. Hence we cannot understand the scientific thought of the seventeenth century without some knowledge of this Aristotelean cosmology and how it came to be challenged.

The essence of the Aristotelean cosmology was its conception of different orders of being and perfection—a conception admirably suited to the structure of a society divided into social orders, each with its divinely ordained duties and a particular sort of virtue and honor. Aristotle made a fundamental distinction between the heavens (everything from the moon upwards) and the sublunar sphere, of which the earth was the center. Everything in the heavens was perfect; nothing ever changed, and all movement described the perfect figure, the circle. Christians had in addition populated the heavens with the hierarchy of angels, memorably located in the spheres of the planets by Dante. On earth matter and motion were imperfect, and indeed it was the degree of imperfection of the matter which explained the quality of the motion. The "essences" of bodies sought their "natural" places in the universe, and the base or "earthy" essence naturally tended to the most ignoble place in the universe, the center of the earth (for Dante, the lowest pit of hell). Upward motion was therefore nobler than downward; this is the explanation of the convention in painting that the top part of the canvas was reserved for the more honorable and important subjects.

The Aristotelean cosmology was perhaps the most comfortable that man has ever conceived. It was built to the human scale and was the natural development of everyday observations and common sense. Critics have suggested that the "organic" power of a mind like Shakespeare's grew out of the ease with which the Aristotelean cosmology fitted human behavior into the cosmic scheme and demonstrated that a deeper order persisted through apparent chaos. But its very encyclopedic character made it vulnerable to attack on a multitude of fronts, and since the middle of the sixteenth century the attack had been pressed home with increasing boldness.

The Overthrow of the Aristotelean Cosmology

Although we conventionally speak of the "Copernican Revolution," it would be less misleading to call it a "Galilean" one. Cosmology as the description of the actual structure and workings of the universe was not at first affected by the writings of the Polish astronomer. Copernicus, as everyone knows, wrote in opposition to the Egyptian astronomer Ptolemy; but Ptolemy had not speculated on the real positions of the earth and sun. He had merely provided a set of mathematical techniques for predicting the motions of the heavenly bodies, based on the assumption that the earth was the center of the universe. (There is thus no "Ptolemaic cosmology.") Because of a preface added by the editor, Copernicus' theories appeared merely in the guise of a rival mathematical theory, saying only that the calculation of the future positions of the heavenly bodies could be made with slightly greater economy of geometrical effort if, for the purposes of the calculation, the sun were hypothesized to be the center of the universe. As a new mathematical hypothesis, Copernicanism seemed relatively innocuous, and indeed it was adopted as the basis of the calendar reform sponsored by the pope himself. Since its comparatively greater mathematical elegance was virtually its only advantage (page 27), it is not surprising that almost all its early supporters were mathematicians.

It was not until the observations of the Danish astronomer Tycho Brahe, using his much larger and thus more accurately calibrated quadrants, and then of Galileo with the telescope that it became clear that Aristotle's picture of the incorruptible heavens filled with impenetrable spheres was incompatible with demonstrable physical fact. And it was Galileo, as both he and Cardinal Bellarmine understood (pages 15 and 17), who was to become the hero and martyr of the real astronomical revolution, because he upheld the Copernican hypothesis as a true description of physical reality and, using the weapons of literature no less than of science, tried to persuade the entire literate public of its truth.

The True Constitution of the Universe

From Galileo, *History and Demonstrations concerning Sunspots* (Rome, 1613). Translated from Italian by Stillman Drake, *Discoveries and Opinions of Galileo* (New York, 1957), pp. 96-97.

I seem to see in Apelles* a free and not a servile mind. He is quite capable of understanding true doctrines. . . . Still, he cannot detach himself entirely from those previously impressed fancies to which his intellect turns back and lends assent from long use and habit. This may be seen once again when he tries to prove that the spots are not in the lunar orb or in those of Venus or Mercury. In doing so he continues to adhere to eccentrics, deferents, equants, epicycles, and the like as if they were real, actual, and distinct things. These, however, are merely assumed by mathematical astronomers in order to facilitate their calculations. They are not retained by philosophical astronomers who, going beyond the demand that they somehow save the appearances, seek to investigate the true constitution of the universe—the most important and most admirable problem that there is. . . .

* A painter who had undertaken to write of astronomical matters against Galileo.

Now I do not deny the existence of circular movements about the earth or other centers, or even circular motions completely separated from the earth and outside its orbit. . . . But that nature, in order to provide these, really makes use of that farrago of spheres and orbs composed by the astronomers is, I think, not so much something we are expected to believe as it is a convenience in astronomical computations.

Our Eyes vs. Aristotle

From Galileo, *Dialogue Concerning the Two Chief World-Systems* (Florence, 1632), second dialogue, pp. 100-101, 105-106. Translated from Italian.

SAGREDO: I found one day in his house a doctor very well thought of in Venice, to whom some came for their studies and others out of curiosity to see dissections performed by an anatomist no less learned than careful and experienced. This day it happened that he was in search of the source and origin of the nerves, about which there is a famous controversy between the Galenist physicians and the Peripatetics.* The anatomist showed how the great strands of nerves leave the brain and, passing down the nape of the neck, extend down the spine and branch through all the body, while only a very fine thread goes to the heart. He then turned to a gentleman whom he knew to be a Peripatetic philosopher, and for whose benefit he had with extraordinary care demonstrated and exhibited everything, and asked him if he was not persuaded and assured that the origin of the nerves comes from the brain and not from the heart. To which the philosopher, after musing a while, responded: "You have made me see this matter so openly and palpably that were it not for the text of Aristotle which asserts the contrary, clearly stating that the nerves originate in the heart, I would be forced to confess your opinion is true."

*   *   *

SIMPLICIO: But when we have abandoned Aristotle, whom shall we have for a guide in philosophy? Nominate some other author.

* Galen (ca. 130-ca. 200 A.D.) was the greatest physiologist of the classical world, and the Galenist texts were regarded as definitive in medicine until the sixteenth century. The Peripatetics were, of course, Aristoteleans.

SALVIATI: We need a guide in unknown or thickly wooded places; but in open and easy country only the blind need a guide, and they should have stayed at home anyway. . . . Don't think I am against listening to Aristotle. I commend the reading and diligent study of him. I only condemn enslaving ourselves to him so far as blindly to subscribe to whatever he says, and without any search for further reasons hold it as an inviolable decree.

Dangers of Irritating Theologians

From a letter of Cardinal Bellarmine to Paolo Antonio Foscarini in Bellarmine, *Works*, XII, 171-172. Translated by Drake, *op. cit.*, pp. 162-163.

. . . It appears to me that Your Reverence and Sig. Galileo did prudently to content yourselves with speaking hypothetically* and not positively, as I have always believed Copernicus did. For to say that assuming the earth moves and the sun stands still saves all the appearances better than eccentrics and epicycles is to speak well. This has no danger in it, and it suffices for mathematicians. But to wish to affirm that the sun is really fixed in the center of the heavens and merely turns upon itself without traveling from east to west, and that the earth is situated in the third sphere and revolves very swiftly around the sun, is a very dangerous thing, not only by irritating all the theologians and scholastic philosophers, but also by injuring our holy faith and making the sacred Scripture false.

An Operatic Universe

From Fontenelle, *On the Plurality of Worlds* (Paris?, 1686), first evening. Translated from French.

All philosophy is grounded on two things: that man has a thirst for knowledge in the mind and poor eyesight. . . . We see

---

* Bellarmine refers to Foscarini's letter to a priest, Sebastian Fantone (1615), in which he answers Biblical objections to Copernicus. Bellarmine soon discovered how prudently Galileo was to confine himself to hypothetical discussions and was instrumental in his first appearance before the Inquisition.

most objects quite otherwise than they are, so that the true philosophers spend their time in not believing what they see and in endeavoring to guess at the knowledge of what they see not; and in my opinion this kind of life is not much to be envied.

I fancy to myself that nature is a great spectacle or play, much like one of our operas. From your seat at the opera you do not see the stage as it really is, since everything is arranged there to present from afar an agreeable appearance, while the wheels and weights which move and counterpoise the machines are all concealed from our view. Nor do we trouble ourselves much to find out how all those motions that we see there are performed; and it may be that there is only one stagehand in the audience who troubles himself with the consideration of how those effects which seem so new and extraordinary to him are managed, and who resolves at any cost to find out the mechanism of them. You will see that this stagehand is not unlike a philosopher; but that which makes the difficulty incomparably greater for philosophers is that in the machinery of nature the ropes are so well hidden that it was a long time before mankind could guess at the causes that moved the vast frame of the universe.

Imagine to yourself the ancient philosophers beholding one of our operas—such ones as Pythagoras, Plato, Aristotle, and many others whose names and reputations make so great a noise in the world—and suppose that they were to behold the flight of Phaeton, who is carried aloft by the winds, and that they could not discern the ropes and pulleys, but were altogether ignorant of the contrivance of the machine behind the scenes. One of them would be apt to say: "It is a certain secret virtue that carries up Phaeton." Another: "Phaeton is composed of certain numbers which make him mount upwards." The third: "Phaeton has a certain affinity for the highest part of the theater and is uneasy when he is not there." And a fourth: "Phaeton was not made for flying, but he would rather fly than leave the upper part of the stage empty"—besides a hundred other notions which I am surprised have not entirely ruined the reputation of the ancients. In our age Descartes, and some other moderns, would say: "Phaeton rises because he is hoisted by ropes, and while he ascends, a greater weight than he descends."

And now men do not believe that any corporeal being moves itself, unless it is set in motion or pushed by another body, or drawn by ropes. . . . And could we see nature as it is, we should see nothing but the hinder part of the theater at the opera.

Bacon and the Strategy of Science

In the very years that Galileo was demonstrating that his new science disproved the basis of the received cosmology, Francis Bacon was calling for a new science without ever embracing the Copernican hypothesis. Throughout a very active political career, which ended in his impeachment as lord chancellor, Bacon had been planning a great project designed to revolutionize all natural philosophy. The Great Instauration, or beginning, he called it. The only parts ever published were *The Advancement of Learning* (1605) and *The New Organon* (1620). The remaining four parts were to consist of reports of experiments. We can get some idea of what he had in mind from the second book of *The New Organon,* where a miscellaneous collection of experiments (and more often only ideas for experiments) on the general subject of "heat" are laid out. In the enforced leisure after his political disgrace, Bacon found time to get out a further volume of experiments, but he despaired of ever collecting enough to be of any use without the generous patronage of a pope or king. Science, he correctly foresaw, had to be "big science," pursued by societies or colleges of inquirers and built up over a long succession of generations.

Since Bacon knew little about Galileo and even slighted the work of the greatest English empirical scientist of his day, William Gilbert, it is obvious that he was not abreast of the best contemporary science. The physician William Harvey commented that Bacon wrote science like a lord chancellor; but it was his philosophical rather than his legal training which provides the key to Bacon's scientific thought. Men are never as original as they think, and this is more true of Bacon than of most. Like Descartes and Hobbes (and Galileo himself, for that matter) Bacon was much more under the influence of Aristotle than he realized; but unlike them, he had not been exposed to the delights and triumphs of geometrical reasoning. Of course, it must be realized that Aristoteleanism was a large part of the mental furniture which every educated man picked up in college or university, while mathematics was not. (Lord Strafford, the great minister of Charles I, was a university graduate but had never learned even simple multiplication.)

It was therefore appropriate that Bacon should think of scientific method as a matter of words, of reforming logic. The old *Organon* was the logic textbook which the Middle Ages had compiled from the works of Aristotle; the *New Organon* must therefore put right the grossness of the syllogism, which was not subtle enough for the phenomena of nature. But Bacon characteristically regarded mathematics as useless in the inquiries he wanted to pursue (page 24); it simply seduced men's minds from the proper study of particular fact into easy but sterile generalizations.

It would be wrong, however, to dismiss Bacon as a figure of little importance in the history of science, even though he was no scientist himself. In the first place, the empirical element in science, though not, as Bacon thought, all-important, was important enough, and likely to be slighted. Next, he was supremely able to articulate the growing mood of impatience with traditional learning; only a widespread discontent could clear the way for replacement by more adequate scientific ideas. Furthermore, Bacon had a remarkable understanding of the institutions and social context required for science to develop. The Royal Society is only one of the monuments to this understanding. We may think that Bacon's vast influence was deserved if we reflect that his greatest gifts were not in philosophy, but in the rarer and perhaps more useful field of prophecy. Though others have given more knowledge, few have given so much hope.

Defects of Traditional Philosophy

From the Preface to Bacon, *The Great Instauration* (London, 1620). Translated from Latin by James Spedding in Bacon, *Works*, IV (London, 1858).

The state of knowledge is not prosperous nor greatly advancing; and . . . a way must be opened for the human understanding entirely different from any hitherto known, and other helps provided in order that the mind may exercise over the nature of things the authority which properly belongs to it.

It seems to me that men do not rightly understand either their store or their strength, but overrate the one and underrate the other. Hence it follows that either from an extravagant estimate of the value of the arts which they possess, they seek no further; or else from too mean an estimate of their own powers they spend their strength in small matters and never put it fairly to the trial in those which go to the main. . . . And since opinion of store is one of the chief causes of want, and satisfaction with the present induces neglect of provision for the future, it becomes a thing not only useful but absolutely necessary that the excess of honor and admiration with which our existing stock of inventions is regarded be in the very entrance and threshold of the work—and that frankly and without circumlocution—stripped off, and men be duly warned not to exaggerate or make too much of them. For let a man look carefully into all that variety of books with which the arts and sciences abound; he will find everywhere endless repetitions of the same thing, varying in the method of treatment, but not new in substance, insomuch that the whole stock, numerous as it appears at first view, proves on examination to be but scanty. And [as] for its value and utility, it must be plainly avowed that the wisdom which we have derived principally from the Greeks is but like the boyhood of knowledge, and has the characteristic property of boys: it can talk, but it cannot generate, for it is fruitful of controversies but barren of works. . . . Observe also that if sciences of this kind had any life in them, that could never have come to pass which has been the case now for many ages—that they stand almost at a stay without receiving any augmentations worthy of the human race . . . and all the tradition and succession of schools is still a succession of masters and scholars, not of inventors and those who bring to further perfection the things invented.

In the mechanical arts we do not find it so; they, on the contrary, as having in them some breath of life, are continually growing and becoming more perfect. As originally invented they are commonly rude, clumsy, and shapeless; afterwards they acquire new powers and more commodious arrangements and constructions, in so far that men shall sooner leave the study and pursuit of them and turn to something else than they arrive at the ultimate perfection of which they are capable. Philosophy and the intellectual sciences, on the contrary, stand like statues, worshipped and celebrated but not moved or advanced. Nay, they sometimes flourish most in the hands of the first author, and afterwards degenerate. . . .

And if there have been any who, not binding themselves either to other men's opinions or to their own, but loving liberty, have desired to engage others along with themselves in search, these, though honest in intention, have been weak in endeavor. For they have been content to follow probable reasons and are carried round in a whirl of arguments, and in the promiscuous liberty of search have relaxed the severity of inquiry. There is none who has dwelt upon experience and the facts of nature as long as is necessary. Some there

are indeed who have committed themselves to the waves of experience
and almost turned mechanics, yet these again have in their very experiments pursued a kind of wandering inquiry, without any regular
system of operations. And besides they have mostly proposed to
themselves certain petty tasks, taking it for a great matter to work
out some single discovery—a course of proceeding at once poor in
aim and unskillful in design. For no man can rightly and successfully investigate the nature of anything in the thing itself; let him
vary his experiments as laboriously as he will, he never comes to a
resting-place, but still finds something to seek beyond. . . . As
for those who have given the first place to logic, supposing that the
surest helps to the sciences were to be found in that, they have indeed most truly and excellently perceived that the human intellect
left to its own course is not to be trusted; but then the remedy is
altogether too weak for the disease, nor is it without evil in itself.
For the logic which is received, though it be very properly applied
to civil business and to those arts which rest in discourse and
opinion, is not nearly subtle enough to deal with nature.

*   *   *

And now . . . I turn to men, to whom I have certain salutary
admonitions to offer and certain fair requests to make. My first ad-
monition . . . is that men confine the sense within the limits of duty
in respect of things divine: for the sense is like the sun, which reveals
the face of earth but seals and shuts up the face of heaven. My next,
that in flying from this evil they fall not into the opposite error,
which they will surely do if they think that the inquisition of nature
is in any part interdicted or forbidden. For it was not that pure and
uncorrupted natural knowledge whereby Adam gave names to the
creatures according to their propriety which gave occasion to the
fall. It was the ambitious and proud desire of moral knowledge to
judge of good and evil, to the end that man may revolt from God
and give laws to himself, which was the form and manner of the
temptation. Whereas of the sciences which regard nature the divine
philosopher declares that "it is the glory of God to conceal a thing,
but it is the glory of the King to find a thing out." Even as though
the divine nature took pleasure in the innocent and kindly sport of
children playing at hide-and-seek and vouchsafed of his kindness
and goodness to admit the human spirit for his playfellow at that
game. . . .

The requests I have to make are these. . . . I entreat men to believe that it is not an opinion to be held, but a work to be done; and
to be well assured that I am laboring to lay the foundation, not of

any sect or doctrine, but of human utility and power. Next, I ask them . . . to come forward themselves and take part in that which remains to be done. Moreover, to be of good hope, nor to imagine that this Instauration of mine is a thing infinite and beyond the power of man, when it is in fact the true end and termination of infinite error; and seeing also that it is by no means forgetful of the conditions of mortality and humanity (for it does not suppose that the work can be altogether completed within one generation, but provides for its being taken up by another); and finally that it seeks for the sciences not arrogantly in the little cells of human wit, but with reverence in the greater world.

Obstacles to the Experimental Method

From Bacon, *New Organon* (London, 1620), Book I, aphorisms 83 and 84. Translated from Latin by James Spedding.

This evil [neglect of proper experiments] has been strangely increased by an opinion or conceit which though of long standing is vain and hurtful; namely, that the dignity of the human mind is impaired by long and close intercourse with experiments and particulars, subject to sense and bound in matter—especially as they are laborious to search, ignoble to meditate, harsh to deliver, illiberal to practice, infinite in number, and minute in subtlety. So that it has come at length to this, that the true way is not merely deserted, but shut out and stopped up—experience being, I do not say abandoned or badly managed, but rejected with disdain.

Again, men have been kept back as by a kind of enchantment from progress in the sciences by reverence for antiquity, by the authority of men accounted great in philosophy, and then by general consent. Of the last I have spoken above.

As for antiquity, the opinion touching it which men entertain is quite a negligent one, and scarcely consonant with the word itself. For the old age of the world is to be accounted the true antiquity; and this is the attribute of our own times, not of that earlier age of the world in which the ancients lived; and which, though in respect of us it was the elder, yet in respect of the world it was the younger. And truly as we look for greater knowledge of human things and a riper judgment in the old man than in the young, because of his experience and of the number and variety of the things which he has seen and heard and thought of, so in like manner from our age, if it but knew its own strength and chose to essay and exert it, much more might fairly be expected than from the ancient times, inasmuch as it is a more advanced age of the world and stored and stocked with infinite experiments and observations.

Nor must it go for nothing that by the distant voyages and travels which have become frequent in our times many things in nature have been laid open and discovered which may let in new light upon philosophy. And surely it would be disgraceful if, while the regions of the material globe—that is, of the earth, of the sea, and of the stars—have been in our times laid widely open and revealed, the intellectual globe should remain shut up within the narrow limits of old discoveries.

And with regard to authority, it shows a feeble mind to grant so much to authors and yet deny time his rights, who is the author of authors, nay rather of all authority. For rightly is truth called the daughter of time, not of authority. . . .

Bacon on Mathematics

From Bacon, *Advancement of Learning* (London, 1965), II, pp. 30-31.

. . . There remains yet another part of natural philosophy which is commonly made a principal part and holds rank with physic special and metaphysics, which is mathematics; but I think it more agreeable to the nature of things and to the light of order to place it as a branch of metaphysics. . . . It is true also that of all other forms (as we understand forms) it is the most abstracted and separable from matter, and therefore most proper to metaphysics, which has likewise been the cause why it has been better labored and inquired [into] than any of the other forms which are more immersed into matter. For it being the nature of the mind of man (to the extreme prejudice of knowledge) to delight in the spacious liberty of generalities, as in a champion region,* and not in the enclosures of particularity . . . mathematics of all other knowledge were the goodliest fields to satisfy that appetite.

* Open and unfenced countryside.

The Development
of "Experimental Philosophy"

It is easy to identify the "Scientific Revolution" with the "discovery of the scientific method," but there is no one scientific method now and certainly there was nothing which can simply be identified as such in the seventeenth century. Many scientists were able to do their work quite successfully without having any very precise philosophical rationale for their methods. Galileo, for example, never set out his famous "resolutive-compositive" method in any systematic fashion and regarded most speculative questions as a waste of time. When he was drawn into them, as in the polemical work *The Assayer,* he states a philosophical position of the first importance (compare pages 31-32 with Descartes, pages 58-61); but it is not a highly self-conscious and thoroughly argued position. Newton's interests turned more naturally to theology and metaphysics, but he half-consciously imported into his physics some of the tenets of the Cambridge Platonists.*

Nevertheless we can speak of a mature style of scientific thought which by the end of the century (largely through its identification with the great name of Newton) was shared by virtually all English scientists and which by the middle of the eighteenth century had even won over most of the French from their allegiance to Descartes. This style of thought is well described by the contemporary name "experimental philosophy," since it was a blending of the mathematical techniques associated with continental rationalism and the experimental skill exemplified by Galileo and the early English scientists. We perhaps have a tendency to exaggerate the importance of the empirical side of seventeenth-century science, and it is well to be reminded of the crudity of the scientific apparatus with which even the greatest experiments were done (page 28) and of the necessarily disagreeable character of many experiments (page 29). Bacon clearly had reason to point out that these dirty and often dangerous experiments were frequently left to the despised artisans and me-

* This is one of the themes of E. A. Burtt's classic *Metaphysical Foundations of Modern Science* (1925).

chanics while the philosopher filled his head with more exalted if less fruitful thoughts.

But there is more to it than this: the lack of proper equipment made a truly experimental resolution of many questions quite impossible. (After all, Kepler's laws were *experimentally* confirmed only in 1957 after the launching of Sputnik I.) The behavior of bodies in cold temperatures, for example, could be studied only on the coldest of midwinter days, as there was no refrigerating machinery. It was similarly impossible to study the behavior of falling bodies in a vacuum, since there were no pumps powerful enough to exhaust the air in the experimenter's vessels. This fact explains why Galileo was so prone to resort to the "thought-experiment."

To Galileo the techniques of geometry provided an ideal space which his mind could master although his instruments were not fully capable of manipulating the real physical world. They also allowed an analysis of natural phenomena that decided which experiments could provide the crucial information. There is no point in experimenting unless the contriver of the experiment knows what it is supposed to prove or disprove. This knowledge had to be reached through mathematics.

Today we would say that there must be a hypothesis preceding the experiment; thus it may seem that Newton, in excluding "hypotheses" from the sphere of science (page 33), is defending the naïve and futile empiricism and total induction of Bacon. But Newton is here objecting to speculations which are taken to be facts without proper verification. Newton owes his supreme accomplishments as a physicist to his combination of mathematical genius and a sense for the crucial experiment, and his method avoids the speculative excesses of Descartes as well as Bacon's verbal physics and manic experimentation.

The Great Book of Philosophy and Its Language

From Galileo, *The Assayer* (Rome, 1623). Translated from Italian by Drake, *op. cit.*, pp. 237-238.

In Sarsi I seem to discern the firm belief that in philosophizing one must support oneself upon the opinion of some celebrated author, as if our minds ought to remain completely sterile and barren unless wedded to the reasoning of some other person. Possibly he thinks that philosophy is a book of fiction by some writer, like the *Iliad* or *Orlando Furioso,* productions in which the least important thing is whether what is written there is true. Well, Sarsi, that is not how matters stand. Philosophy is written in this grand book, the universe, which stands continually open to our gaze. But the book cannot be understood unless one first learns to comprehend the language and read the letters in which it is composed. It is written in the language of mathematics, and its characters are triangles, circles, and other geometric figures without which it is humanly impossible to understand a single word of it; without these, one wanders about in a dark labyrinth.

Reason Rapes the Senses

From Galileo, *Dialogue concerning the Two Chief World-Systems* (Florence, 1632), third dialogue, p. 325. Translated from Italian.

SALVIATI: You marvel, Sagredo, that so few are members of the sect which adheres to the Pythagorean opinion. Quite on the contrary, I am surprised that there are any who have embraced and followed it, and I cannot sufficiently admire the pre-eminence of those men's minds who have received it and held it to be true, and by the power of their intellects offered such violence to their own senses as to prefer that which reason dictated to them over that which palpable experience most clearly showed to the contrary. We have already seen that the reasons against the daily revolution of the earth which you have examined have great plausibility . . . but those which openly contradict the annual motion are still of so much more force that (I say again) I cannot find bounds for my admiration how the reason of Aristarchus and Copernicus has committed such a rape upon their senses* as despite them to make herself mistress of their belief.

* Literally, has done violence to their senses. The more lurid phrase is from Salusbury's translation (1665).

Triumphs of the Experimenter

From Galileo, *Discourses and Mathematical Demonstrations concerning Two New Sciences pertaining to Mechanics and Local Motion* (Leiden, 1638). Translated from Italian.

SIMPLICIO: This simple and clear discourse of Sagredo pleases me more than the Author's* more obscure demonstration . . . but I still question whether this is the acceleration which Nature makes use of in the motion of descending heavy bodies; and therefore, so that I and others like me may more clearly understand this, I think it would be appropriate, before we go on, to produce some of those experiments—which are said to be numerous—which agree with the conclusions demonstrated.

SALVIATI: You, like a person of true skill, make a very reasonable demand; for it is usual and convenient to do so in sciences that apply mathematical demonstrations to physical conclusions, as is seen in those that treat perspective, astronomy, mechanics, music, and others, where tangible experiments confirm the fundamental principles of the subject. Therefore I hope it will not be thought superfluous if we discourse at some length upon this first and great foundation, on which lies the weight of the immense structure of infinite conclusions, only a small part of which are mentioned in this book by our author, who thought it enough to open the door that has hitherto been shut to inquiring minds. As to experiments, the author made several; and to assure us that the acceleration of descending heavy bodies conforms to the formula specified above, I have often made with him the following trial:

We took a wooden plank about twenty feet long, a foot wide, and about three finger-breadths thick, and made in one edge a groove a little wider than a finger, which we planed so as to make it straight and smooth. To make it even smoother we glued in it a piece of parchment polished as smooth as possible. In this groove we let roll a very hard, round, and smooth brass ball. Then, raising the plank at pleasure a yard or two above the plane of the horizon, we let the ball descend along the groove, observing (in the manner I shall soon describe) the time it spent in running from top to bottom.

We repeated this often, in order to be certain of the amount of

* Galileo

time spent in the descent, and in these times we never found any perceptible variation, even as much as a tenth of one pulse-beat. Having accurately established this, we let the ball descend only a fourth of the length of the groove; and measuring the time of its descent, we found it to be exactly half of the other. And then experimenting with other lengths, comparing them with the time taken for the whole . . . by experiments repeated nearly a hundred times, we always found the spaces to be to one another as the squares of the times, no matter what was the inclination of the plane (that is, the groove down which the ball rolled). . . .

Now as to the measuring of time: we hung up a large bucket of water with a very small hole in the bottom, through which a small jet of water spurted, which we caught in a small cup during the time that the ball was rolling down the groove. The amounts of water thus collected were weighed each time in a very exact balance, and the differences and proportions of their weights showed exactly the differences and proportions of the time, with (as I said) only negligible variations.

Problems of the Experimenter

From a letter of Robert Hooke to Robert Boyle (1664) in Boyle, *Works* (London, 1772), VI, p. 498.

The other experiment (which I shall hardly, I confess, make again, because it was cruel) was with a dog, which, by means of a pair of bellows wherewith I filled his lungs and suffered them to empty again, I was able to preserve alive as long as I could desire, after I had wholly opened the thorax. . . . Nay, I kept him alive above an hour after I had cut off the pericardium and the mediastinum, and had handled and turned his lungs and heart and all the other parts of its body as I pleased. My design was to make some inquiries into the nature of respiration. But . . . I could not make the least discovery of what I longed for, which was to see if I could by any means discover a passage of the air out of the lungs into either the vessels or the heart; and I shall hardly be induced to make any further trials of this kind, because of the torture of the creature; but certainly the inquiry would be very noble if we could any way find a way so to stupefy the creature as that it might not be sensible, which I fear there is hardly any opiate will perform.

One Experiment Is Enough

From a letter by Newton in *Philosophical Transactions,* 128 (1676), pp. 702-703.

Concerning Mr. Lucas's other experiments [about optics] I am much obliged to him that he would take these things so far into consideration and be at so much pains for examining them; and I thank him so much the more because he is the first that has sent me an experimental examination of them. By this I may presume he really desires to know what truth there is in these matters. But yet it will conduce to his more speedy and full satisfaction if he a little change the method he has propounded, and instead of a multitude of things try only the *Experimentum Crucis.** For it is not number of experiments, but weight to be regarded; and where one will do, what need many?

Had I thought more requisite, I could have added more. . . . And as for the experiments set down in my first letter to you, they were only such as I thought convenient to select. . . .

The main thing he goes about to examine is the different refrangibility of light. And this I demonstrated by the *Experimentum Crucis.* Now if this demonstration be good, there needs no further examination of the thing; if not, the fault of it is to be shown, for the only way to examine a demonstrated proposition is to examine the demonstration. Let that experiment therefore be examined in the first place, and that which it proves be acknowledged, and then if Mr. Lucas wants my assistance to unfold the difficulties which he fancies to be in the experiments he has propounded, he shall freely have it; for then I suppose a few words may make them plain to him—whereas should I be drawn from demonstrative experiments to begin with those it might create us both the trouble of a long dispute, and by the multitude of words cloud rather than clear up the truth. For if it has already cost us so much trouble to agree upon the matter of fact in the first and plainest experiment, and yet we are not fully agreed, what an endless trouble might it create us if we should give ourselves up to dispute upon every argument that occurs; and what should become of Truth in such a tedious dispute?

* Literally, crucial experiment. Newton leaves it in Latin because he evidently considers it a technical term.

Sensations and the "Primary Qualities" of Matter

From Galileo, *The Assayer* (Rome, 1623). Translated from Italian by Drake, *op. cit.*, pp. 274-277.

First I must consider what it is that we call heat, as I suspect that people in general have a concept of this which is very remote from the truth. For they believe that heat is a real phenomenon, or property, or quality, which actually resides in the material by which we feel ourselves warmed. Now I say that whenever I conceive any material or corporeal substance, I immediately feel the need to think of it as bounded and as having this or that shape; as being large or small in relation to other things, and in some specific place at any given time; as being in motion or at rest; as touching or not touching some other body; and as being one in number, or few, or many. From these conditions I cannot separate such a substance by any stretch of my imagination. But that it must be white or red, bitter or sweet, noisy or silent, and of sweet or foul odor, my mind does not feel compelled to bring in as necessary accompaniments. Without the senses as our guides, reason or imagination unaided would probably never arrive at qualities like these. Hence I think that tastes, odors, colors, and so on are no more than mere names so far as the object in which we place them is concerned, and that they reside only in the consciousness. Hence if the living creature were removed, all these qualities would be wiped away and annihilated. But since we have imposed upon them special names, distinct from those of the other and real qualities mentioned previously, we wish to believe that they really exist as actually different from those.

I may be able to make my notion clearer by means of some examples. I move my hand first over a marble statue and then over a living man. As to the effect flowing from my hand, this is the same with regard to both objects and my hand; it consists of the primary phenomena of motion and touch, for which we have no further names. But the live body which receives these operations feels different sensations according to the various places touched. When touched upon the soles of the feet, for example, or under the knee or armpit, it feels in addition to the common sensation of touch a sensation on which we have imposed a special name, "tickling." This sensation belongs to us and not to the hand. Anyone would make a serious error if he said that the hand, in addition to the properties of moving and touching, possessed another faculty of "tickling," as if tickling were a phenomenon that resided in the hand that tickled. A piece of paper or a feather drawn lightly over any part of our bodies performs intrinsically the same operations of moving and touching, but by touching the eye, the nose, or the upper lip it excites in us an almost intolerable titillation, even though elsewhere it is scarcely felt. This titillation belongs entirely to us and not to the feather; if the live and sensitive body were removed it would remain no more than a mere word. I believe that no more solid an existence belongs to many qualities which we have come to attribute to physical bodies—tastes, odors, colors, and many more

* * *

To excite in us tastes, odors, and sounds I believe that nothing is required in external bodies except shapes, numbers, and slow or rapid movements. I think that if ears, tongues, and noses were removed, shapes and numbers and motions would remain, but not odors or tastes or sounds. The latter, I believe, are nothing more than names when separated from living beings, just as tickling and titillation are nothing but names in the absence of such things as noses and armpits. . . .

Having shown that many sensations which are supposed to be qualities residing in external objects have no real existence save in us, and outside ourselves are mere names, I now say that I am inclined to believe heat to be of this character. Those materials which produce heat in us and make us feel warmth, which are known by the general name of "fire," would then be a multitude of minute particles having certain shapes and moving with certain velocities. Meeting with our bodies, they penetrate by means of their extreme subtlety, and their touch as felt by us when they pass through our substance is the sensation we call "heat."

Science Perfected in Becoming Mathematical

From the preface to Newton, *Mathematical Principles of Natural Philosophy* (London, 1687). Translated from Latin by Andrew Motte (London, 1729).

Since the Ancients (as we are told by Pappus) made great account of the science of mechanics in the investigation of natural things, and the Moderns, laying aside substantial forms and occult qualities, have endeavored to subject the phenomena of nature to the laws of mathematics, I have in this treatise cultivated mathematics so far as it regards philosophy. . . . For all the difficulty of philosophy seems to consist in this: from the phenomena of motions to investigate the forces of Nature, and then from these forces to demonstrate the other phenomena. . . . By the propositions mathematically demonstrated in the first books, we there derive from the celestial phenomena the forces of gravity with which bodies tend to the sun and the several planets. Then from these forces by other propositions which are also mathematical we deduce the motions of the planets, the comets, the moon, and the sea. I wish we could derive the rest of the phenomena of nature by the same kind of reasoning from mechanical principles. For I am induced by many reasons to suspect that they may all depend upon certain forces by which the particles of bodies, by some causes hitherto unknown, are either mutually impelled towards each other and cohere in regular figures, or are repelled and recede from each other; which forces being unknown, philosophers have hitherto attempted the search of nature in vain. But I hope the principles here laid down will afford some light either to that or some truer method of philosophy.

Newton's Method

From Newton, *Optics*, 2nd. ed. (London, 1718), Book III, queries.

As in mathematics, so in natural philosophy the investigation of difficult things by the method of analysis ought ever to precede the method of composition. This analysis consists in making experiments and observations, and in drawing general conclusions from them by induction, and admitting of no objections against the conclusions but such as are taken from experiments or other certain truths. For hypotheses are not to be regarded in experimental philosophy. And although the arguing from experiments and observations by induction be no demonstration of general conclusions, yet it is the best way of arguing which the nature of things admits of, and may be looked upon as so much the stronger by how much the induction is more general. And if no exception occur from phenomena, the conclusion may be pronounced generally. But if at any time afterwards any exception shall occur from experiments, it may then begin to be pronounced with such exceptions as occur. By this way of analysis we may proceed from compounds to ingredients and from motions to the forces producing them, and in general from effects to their causes and from particular causes to more general ones, till the argument end in the most general. This is the method of analysis; and the synthesis consists in assuming the causes discovered and established as principles, and by them explaining the phenomena proceeding from them and proving the explanations.

Social Mathematics

It is not surprising that the intoxicating successes of science and mathematics should have recommended them not only to philosophers but also to historians and to the newly emerging political economists. Thus far we have emphasized the attractions of geometry; but another contemporary mathematical achievement, probability theory, was more immediately relevant to religion (pages 161-4) and politics. Probability calculations made possible, for example, that more dignified form of gambling which we call insurance (the first life insurance policy was written in the seventeenth century). It is hard to exaggerate the importance which insurance has had for the development of modern society, since it brought hazards much more nearly under rational control by, in effect, socializing them.

Not all mathematical applications were destined to such a long and happy life, as we may see from the excerpts from the Reverend John Craig (page 35). It now seems a rare folly to compute the half-life of faith, on the best Newtonian lines, but Craig must at least have the glory of being a typical fool. His folly is instructive in that it only carries to somewhat enthusiastic lengths the general confidence in that new science by which, now, "all was light."

The Method of Political Arithmetic

From Sir William Petty, *Political Arithmetic* (London, 1690), preface.

The method I take . . . is not yet very usual, for instead of using only comparative and superlative words and intellectual arguments, I have taken the course (as a specimen of the political arithmetic I have long aimed at) to express myself in terms of number, weight, or measure; to use only arguments of sense, and to consider only such causes as have visible foundations in nature; leaving those that depend upon the mutable minds, opinions, appetites, and passions of particular men to the consideration of others. . . .

Probability Theory as an Intellectual Tool

From the translator's preface to Christiaan Huygens, *The Laws of Chance* (London, 1692). Original in Latin (1657).

The reader may here observe the force of numbers, which can be successfully applied even to those things which one would imagine are subject to no rules. There are very few things which we know which are not capable of being reduced to a mathematical reasoning; and when they cannot, it is a sign our knowledge of them is very small and confused. And where a mathematical reasoning can be had, it is as great folly to make use of any other as to grope for a thing in the dark when you have a candle standing by you. I believe the calculation of the quantity of probability might be improved to a very useful and pleasant speculation and applied to a great many events which are accidental, besides those of games; only these cases would be infinitely more confused, as depending on chances which the most part of men are ignorant of. . . . All the politics in the world are nothing else but a kind of analysis of the quantity of probability in casual events, and a good politican signifies no more than one who is dextrous at such calculations; only the principles which are made use of in the solution of such problems can't be studied in a closet, but acquired by the observation of mankind.

Mathematics of Faith and Probability

From John Craig, *Mathematical Principles of Christian Theology* (London, 1699). Translated from Latin in *History and Theory*, Beiheft 4 (1963).

Prop. II. Theor. II
Historical probability increases in proportion to the number of primary witnesses who describe the event.

*   *   *

Corollary. Let there be any history H, related to any man A by any number of first witnesses $n + m$, of whom only some say, n, describe the same history to another man B; the probability which A has will be to the probability which B has as $n + m$ to n.

Prop. III, Theor. III

Suspicions of historical probability transmitted through single successive witnesses (other things being equal) increase in proportion to the numbers of witnesses through whom the history is handed down.

Let s be the total suspicion which we have concerning the trustworthiness and other virtues of an ideal witness; then if one witness should give s, two witnesses will give $2s$, three witnesses will give $3s$; and universally a number of n witnesses will give ns suspicions. . . .

Prop. IV. Lemma I

Velocity of suspicion produced in equal periods of time increases in arithmetical progression. . . .

Prop. XVII. Probl[em] X

To determine the degree of the present probability of the story of Christ written by four historians, and transmitted through one series of exemplars.

The present probability of the story of Christ is $cz + (n - 1)f + \dfrac{T^2k}{t^2}$. . . .

In this case the number of first historians c is equal to 4, T is equal to 1696 years 34t. . . .

Prop. XVIII. Probl[em] XI

To define the space of time in which the probability of the written History of Christ will vanish.

That probability will vanish when $cz + (n - 1)f + \dfrac{T^2k}{t^2} = 0$. . . .

this equation when reduced will give the required time of vanishing probability, namely $T = t\sqrt{\left(4001 + \dfrac{1}{64}\right)} - \dfrac{10}{8}t$, or . . . 3150 years. . . .

Corollary. It is necessary that Christ come before 1454 years elapse. For it is necessary that Christ come before the probability of the Gospel story vanishes; but that probability will perish when 1454 years ($= 3150 - 1696$) have elapsed from our time. . . . And in no time less than 1454 years is it necessary for him to come, insofar as his arrival depends upon the disappearance of the probability of his history. And certainly many things move me to suspect that he will not come before the probability of his history has nearly vanished;

for it is this that Luke seems expressly to hint at in Chapter 18, Verse 8, of his Gospel, where he relates that Christ demanded in this manner—*"Nevertheless when the son of man cometh, shall he find faith on the earth?"*—so little, that is, will be the probability of his story at the coming of Christ that he doubts whether he will find anyone who will give faith to this history concerning himself. Whence it is apparent how gravely in error are all those who fix the coming of Christ so near to our times.

Part III

DESCARTES' SEARCH
FOR METHOD

Introduction

A few generations in the history of Europe have been possessed by the idea that the whole of human knowledge would open to them if only some new intellectual tool were put in use. In the early twelfth century, dialectic was the tool which would of itself generate truth; in the late fifteenth, it was knowledge of Greek which would restore the full glory of classical civilization, so long corrupted by barbarous translations and commentaries. The early seventeenth century was once again haunted by the combination of acute dissatisfaction with the state of knowledge and simple faith in a new technique. Bacon was the prophet of this mood, but he suffered the customary prophetic fate and was not allowed to enter the Promised Land. That seemed to have been reserved for René Descartes.

Bacon is almost the only philosopher of whom Descartes speaks with generosity or even respect, but he praises his hopes and not his thoughts. The men were very different. Descartes fled the cares and rewards of high office as enthusiastically as Bacon pursued them. His inheritance from his father, a member of the French order of legal nobility, left Descartes the means to retire at the age of thirty to the Netherlands, where, he commented, his fellow citizens were so eagerly making their fortunes that they had no time to pester him.

In one of the first pieces he ever wrote, Descartes compared himself to a masked actor—two steps removed, in other words, from full participation in real life. He is not a self-revealing writer, and the *Discourse on Method* is not really an autobiography, although it looks like one. (It was in fact published anonymously, though Descartes had to acknowledge that he had written it.) Nor is the *Discourse* the best statement of his general philosophical position; it contains an important contradiction in the fourth part which has to be resolved by appeal to his other works. But it is by far the most important historical document that Descartes wrote, because it best explains why he was able to have such an influence on the style of thought and life of his contemporaries.

When Pascal coined the phrase *esprit géométrique*—"mathmatical mind" is perhaps the nearest English equivalent—it was principally Descartes whom he had in mind. For Descartes shows in its purest form the faith that, since all minds are substantially equal, it is the geometrical method of reasoning, proceeding by deduction from the clearest and most obvious truths, which alone can lead men to philosophical discoveries. It is true that Descartes liked to sound less radical than he was, but no attentive reader can miss the revolutionary implications of calling all knowledge before the bar to be judged by the Cartesian method.*

Consider his dismissal of traditional scholarship. He thought Greek was suitable only for schoolboy exercises and counted himself lucky to have forgotten what little of it he had learned. History could offer little more, since Descartes made a radical attack on the credibility of tradition. Certainty, he argues, can reside only in consciousness of the rational process by which a proposition is deduced from indubitable truths. Memory is thus worthless as a source of knowledge. In fact, the reason the mind is ridden with error is that it remembers what has been taught by those unsatisfactory pedagogues, the schoolmasters and the passions of our childhood. The first necessity is therefore to subject all these remnants of childish error to the purgation of systematic doubt, so that the remaining certainties can be used as the foundation for the subsequent structure of truth.

The experience which lies behind the *Discourse on Method* was a series of dreams which Descartes had on the night of November 10, 1619. The first two of these dreams were menacing ones, which he interpreted as God reproving him for his sins; but the third was more benign, and Descartes took it as conveying the seal of divine approval for his mathematical philosophy. He continued to cherish this experience somewhat like the memory of a religious conversion, and his account of it in the first parts of the Discourse inevitably reminds us—despite his repeated disclaimers that he is recommending any of

* An adjective coined from the Latin form of his name (which he greatly disliked).

his experiences as a model for anyone else—of those confessional accounts of conversions which were so often used for evangelistic purposes by the radical sects. The temper of Descartes' mind was not really skeptical; his genius was for faith and not for doubt.

The particular arguments and tenets of Descartes' philosophy were often the starting points for all future philosophical investigations, and the textbooks are doubtless correct, if there is a need to establish paternity, in calling him the father of modern philosophy. But besides his explicit philosophy there was an ill-defined body of beliefs and attitudes which spread far beyond the professional philosophers and came to influence, to some degree, almost every educated man. This protean "Cartesianism," more than any precise apprehension of his doctrines, constituted the enormous influence of Descartes in the latter part of the seventeenth century, an influence which even now has not been exhausted. (It is doubtful that Jean-Paul Sartre will be the last of the Cartesians.) We can perhaps understand this better by pondering the nearest historical parallel of our own times, Freudianism; for Freud and Descartes may be taken as founders of what must be called rationalist religions. Both put a similar emphasis on recovering rational control over the parts of the mind which were still dominated by childhood beliefs (though Descartes' model of the mind was much simpler). Both seemed to speak for a way of life which would be morally satisfying because it was in harmony with the latest scientific thought (though the scientific work of both now looks rather less impressive than it did at the time). Cartesianism is perhaps the first demonstration that Europe in times of acute cosmological crisis would no longer turn to priests in its perplexity.

Descartes' Account of His Education

From Descartes, *Discourse on Method* (Leiden, 1637), Part I. Translated from French.

Good sense is the most equally divided thing in the world; for everyone believes himself so well supplied with it that even those who in all other things are the hardest to please seldom desire more of it than they have. In this it is not likely that all men are deceived; it rather shows that the faculty of judging well and distinguishing the true from the false, which is properly called good sense or reason, is by nature equal in all men. Thus the diversity of our opinions comes not because some men are more reasonable than others, but only because we direct our thoughts along different paths and do not consider the same things. For it is not enough to have a good mind; the principal thing is to apply it well. The greatest souls are as capable of the greatest vices as of the most eminent virtues; so those who move very slowly may advance much farther if they always follow the right way than those who run but stray from it.

For my part, I never presumed that my mind was more perfect in anything than an ordinary man's; nay, I have often wished to have thoughts as quick, or an imagination as clear and distinct, or a memory as ample and as ready, as some other men have had . . .

But I shall not fear to say that I believe myself very happy in having . . . found a method by which, it seems to me, I have the means to augment by degrees my knowledge and little by little to raise it to the highest pitch which the meanness of my capacity and the short course of my life can permit it to attain. For I have already gathered such fruits from it that—although in the judgment I make of myself I try always to incline to diffidence rather than to presumption, and, as I look on the various actions and undertakings of all men with the eye of a philosopher, there is almost none which does not seem to me vain and useless—I am nevertheless extremely satisfied with the progress which (it seems to me) I have already made in the search for truth and do conceive such hopes for the future that if, among the employments of men purely as men there is some one that is solidly good and important, I dare believe it is that which I have chosen.

Yet it may be that I deceive myself, and perhaps it is but a little copper and glass which I take for gold and diamonds. I know how subject we are to mistake in those things which concern us and how suspicious we ought to be of the judgment of our friends when it is in our favor. But I should willingly in this discourse show you the ways which I have followed, and set forth my life as in a picture so that everyone may judge it. And, learning from the common reaction what men's opinions of it are, I may find a new means of instructing myself which I shall add to those I customarily make use of.

Thus it is not my design to teach a method which every man ought to follow for the good conduct of his reason, but only to show in what manner I have endeavored to order my own. Those who undertake to give precepts ought to consider themselves more clever than those to whom they give them, and they are culpable of they fail in the slightest matter. But I propose this discourse only as a history or, if you will, only as a fable wherein, among other examples which may be imitated, one may perhaps find several others which it would be wrong for him to follow. So I hope it will be profitable to some without being hurtful to any and that its frankness will earn the gratitude of everyone.

I have been bred up to letters from my infancy, and because I was persuaded that by means of them a man might acquire a clear and certain knowledge of all that is useful for this life, I was extremely desirous to learn them. But as soon as I had finished all the course of my studies, at the end of which men are usually received into the ranks of the learned, I wholly changed my opinion; for I found myself entangled in so many doubts and errors that it seemed to me I had made no other profit in seeking to instruct myself except that I had more and more discovered my own ignorance. Yet I was in one of the most famous schools in Europe* where I thought, if there were any on earth, there ought to have been learned men. I had learned all that the others had learned, and being unsatisfied with the sciences which were taught us, I had even read over all the books which I could possibly procure treating such as are held to be the most rare and curious. I knew the judgment others made of me, and I perceived that I was no less esteemed than my fellow students, although there were some among them that were destined to succeed to our masters' places. And finally, our age seemed to me as flourishing and as fertile in good minds as any of the preceding ones, which made me take the liberty to judge all other men by my own measure and to conclude that there was no such learning in the world as I had formerly been led to hope.

Yet I continued to esteem the exercises of the schools. I knew that the languages which are learned there are necessary for the understanding of ancient books; that the prettiness of fables awakens the mind; that the memorable actions in history elevate it, and that, if read with discretion, they help to form the judgment; that the reading of all good books is like a conversation with the most well-bred persons of the past age who were the authors of them—in fact, a studied conversation, wherein they disclose to us only the best of their thoughts. I knew that eloquence has force and beauty which is incomparable; that poetry has very ravishing delicacies and sweetness; that mathematics has most subtle inventions, which very much serve both to satisfy the curious and to facilitate all the arts and lessen the labor of men; that those writings which deal with morals contain several teachings and exhortations to virtue which are very useful; that theology teaches how to gain heaven; that philosophy affords us the means to speak plausibly of all things and gets the admiration

* The college of La Flèche.

even of the least learned men; that law, medicine, and the other sciences bring honor and riches to those who practice them; and finally that it is good to have examined them all, even the falsest and most superstitious, so that we may discover their just value and be on our guard against their deceptions.

But I thought I had spent time enough with the languages, and even in the reading of the histories and fables of ancient books. For conversing with those of former ages is much like travel. It is good to know something of the manners of several nations, so that we may judge our own more sensibly and not think that all things against our mode are ridiculous or unreasonable, as men who have seen nothing usually do. But when we employ too long a time in travel, we at last become strangers to our own country; and when we are too curious about those things which were practiced in former times, we commonly remain very ignorant of those which are now in use. Besides, fables make us imagine some events possible which are not so, and even the most faithful histories, though they neither change nor augment the value of things in order to make them more worth reading about, nevertheless almost always omit the basest and least remarkable circumstances, which makes the rest seem otherwise than it is—so that those who order their lives by the examples which they draw from these histories are prone to fall into the extravagancies of the Paladins of our romances and to conceive designs beyond their abilities.

I highly prized eloquence and was in love with poetry, but I thought of both as gifts of the mind rather than as the fruits of study. Those who have the strongest reasoning powers and who best digest their thoughts in order to render them more clear and intelligible can always in this way make their case more strongly, although they speak only a dialect like Breton and have never learned rhetoric; and those whose inventions are most pleasing and who can express them with most ornament and sweetness will still be the best poets, although ignorant of the art of poetry.

Beyond everything I was most pleased with mathematics, because of the certainty and evidence of its reasoning; but I had not yet discovered its true use and, thinking it was useful only for mechanical pursuits, I was surprised that nothing more sublime had been built upon grounds which were so firm and solid. On the contrary, I compared the writings of the ancient pagans which treated ethics to most proud and stately palaces which were built only on sand and mud. They exalt the virtues very highly and make them appear more estimable than everything in the world, but they do not sufficiently instruct us in the knowledge of them; and often what they give a fair name is only a stupid blunder, or an act of pride or of despair, or a parricide.

I reverenced our theology and laid claim to gaining heaven as much as anyone; but having learned as a most certain truth that the way to it is no less open to the most ignorant than to the most learned and that those revealed truths which lead thither are beyond our understanding, I dared not submit them to the weakness of my reasoning. Also I thought that a successful examination of them required some extraordinary assistance from heaven, to someone who could be more than a mere man.

I shall say only this of philosophy: seeing that it has been cultivated by the most excellent intellects that have lived in these many ages, and nevertheless there is nothing in it which is not disputed (and consequently not doubtful) I could not presume to hope to succeed better than others. And, considering how many different opinions learned men may maintain on the same matter, although only one of them can be true, I held all to be false which were no more than probable.

As for the other sciences, since they borrow their principles from philosophy, I judged that nothing solid could be built upon such unsound foundations, and neither honor nor wealth could induce me to study them. For (thank God) I did not feel myself in a condition which obliged me to make a trade of science for the relief of my fortune. And, though I did not profess to despise glory as the cynics do, yet I put very little value on what I could acquire only by false pretenses. And lastly, as for false teachings, I thought I already knew too well what they were to be deceived any further by the promises of an alchemist, the predictions of an astrologer, the impostures of a magician, or by the conceits and bragging of those who profess to know more than they do.

This is why, as soon as my years freed me from subjection to my tutors, I wholly gave up the study of letters; and, resolving to seek no other knowledge but what I could find in myself or in the great book of the world, I employed the rest of my youth in travel, in seeing courts and armies, frequenting people of different temperaments and conditions, and, to gain experience, in testing myself in such encounters of fortune as might occur, everywhere making reflection on those things which presented themselves to me so that I could draw some profit from them. For it seemed to me that I could meet with far more truth in the reasoning which every man makes about the affairs which concern him, where the result would quickly punish him if he had judged amiss, than in those which a literary man makes in his study concerning speculations which produce no

effect and are of no consequence to him—except that perhaps he
may gain more occasions for vanity the more they are removed from
the common understanding, since he must have employed more wit
and subtlety in attempting to render them plausible. In everything,
I had always an extreme desire to learn to distinguish the true from
the false, in order to see clearly into my actions and pass this life
with assurance.

It is true that while I only considered the manners of other men,
I found little or nothing which could serve as a firm basis for my
own; and I observed as much diversity of manners as I had found
before in the opinions of the philosophers. Hence the greatest profit
I could reap from them was that, seeing that several things which
seem to us very peculiar and ridiculous are nevertheless commonly
received and approved by other great nations, I learned to believe
nothing too firmly which I had been persuaded of only by example
or by custom. And thus little by little I freed myself from many errors which can eclipse our natural light and render us less able to
comprehend reason. But after I had employed some years in thus
studying the book of the world and endeavoring to get experience, I
made one day a resolution to study also within myself and to employ
all the forces of my mind in choosing the way I should follow. In
this, I think, I succeeded much better than if I had never left my
country or my books.

Rules of the Method

From *Discourse on Method,* Part II.

I was then* in Germany, where I had been called by the
wars which are still going on there. As I was returning to the army
from the Emperor's coronation, the onset of winter caught me at a
place where, finding no conversation to divert me, and moreover
having by good fortune no cares or passions to trouble me, I stayed
alone for a whole day shut up [as if] in a stove, where I had leisure
enough to entertain myself with my thoughts.

Among these one of the first that I pondered was that often there
is less perfection in work composed of several pieces and made by the
hands of different masters than in those that were made by one only.

* 1619

Thus we may observe that those buildings which were undertaken and finished by one architect only are commonly more beautiful and better ordered than those which several have labored to patch up, making use of old walls which were built for other purposes. Thus those ancient cities which, beginning only as villages, become in the passage of time great towns are usually ugly and sprawling in comparison with other regular places which a designer may arrange according to his fancy on a clear site. Although, considering their buildings separately, we often find as much or more art in the first, yet when we see how they are arranged, here a great one, there a little one, and how they make the streets crooked and uneven, we must say that it is chance rather than the will of men using their reason that has so placed them. . . . So also I imagined that those peoples who had at one time been half savage and who became civilized only by degrees have made their laws only in response to the inconveniences arising from their crimes and quarrels, and could not have so good a form of government as those who from the beginning of their association observed the constitution of some prudent legislator. Also it is equally certain that the state of the true religion, whose ordinances God alone has made, must be incomparably better regulated than all others. And, to speak of human affairs, I believe that if Sparta at one time greatly flourished, it was not because of the virtue of any one of their laws in particular—many of them being very strange and even immoral—but because, having been invented by one man only, they all tended to the same end. And so I thought that the learning in books—at least those whose arguments are only probable and which have no demonstration—being composed and enlarged upon little by little with the opinions of several persons, comes not so near the truth as those simple reasonings which a man of good sense can naturally make touching those things which he encounters. Furthermore, I thought that since we have all been children before becoming men and necessarily have been governed for a long time by our appetites and by our tutors, which were often contrary to one another (and neither of which, perhaps, always counselled us for the best) it is almost impossible that our judgments could be so clear or so solid as they might have been if we had had the full use of our reason from the time of our birth and had always been guided by it alone.

It is true that we do not see the houses of a whole town pulled down just to rebuild them in another style and to make the streets more beautiful; but we often see men pull down their own in order to reconstruct them, and even sometimes they are forced to do so, when they are in danger of falling of their own weight and when their foundations are not sound. From this example I persuaded

myself that it was senseless for a private person to design the reformation of a state, changing everything from the very foundations and
overturning in order to redress; or, equally, to reform the bodies of
knowledge and the established curricula in the schools for teaching
them. But for all the opinions to which I had until then given cre-
dence, I could not do better than to undertake to expunge them
once and for all, in order either to put better ones in their place or
else the same ones again as soon as I had squared them with reason.
And I was confident that by this means I should succeed much better in the conduct of my life than if I had built only on old foundations and relied only on those principles of which I allowed myself
to be persuaded in my youth, without ever having examined the
truth of them. For, although I observed several difficulties in my
project, they were not without remedy and were not at all compara-
ble to those which occur in the reformation of the least things pertaining to the public. . . .

As for the imperfections [of states], if they have any—as we know
that many must have them, just from the differences between them
—custom has doubtless much softened them and has even avoided
or insensibly corrected many which we could not have remedied so
well by reason. In short they are almost always more tolerable than
changing them could be, in the same way that great roads winding
between mountains become little by little, through being so much
used, so smooth and commodious that it is better to follow them
than to try to go in a straight line by climbing over the rocks and descending to the bottom of precipices.

Therefore I can by no means approve of those turbulent and un-
quiet spirits who, being called neither by birth nor by fortune to the
management of public affairs, yet are always forming, in theory, some
new reformation. And if I thought there was the least thing in this
discourse by which I could be suspected of that folly, I should be
extremely sorry to allow it to be published. I never had any design
which extended further than to reform my own thoughts and to
build them on a foundation which is wholly mine. . . .

In my youth I had studied, among the divisions of philosophy, a
little logic, and in mathematics, algebra and the analyses of geometers. These three arts or sciences, it seemed, ought to contribute
something to my design. But on examination I became aware that
logic in its syllogisms and most of its other lessons serves rather to
explain to other people what we already know—or even, like Lull's
art,* to speak without judgment of the things that we are ignorant

* Magic of a cabbalistic sort, depending on spells and incantations, supposedly
practiced by the Spanish philosopher and rhetorician Raymond Lull (ca. 1235-
1315).

of rather than learn them. And although it contains in fact many very true and good precepts, yet there are a great many others mixed among them which are either hurtful or superfluous, so that it is as difficult to separate them as to draw a Diana or a Minerva out of a block of marble which is not yet rough-hewn. Next, as for the analysis of the ancients and the algebra of the moderns, besides extending only to very abstract and apparently useless matters, the former seems so limited to the consideration of figures that it cannot exercise the understanding without very much tiring the imagination; and in the latter we are so much subjected to certain rules and numbers that algebra has been made a confused and obscure art which perplexes the mind instead of a science which instructs it. For this reason I thought I ought to seek some other method which, profiting from the advantages of these, might be exempt from their defects. And as the multitude of laws often furnishes excuses for vice, so that a state is far better governed when it has only a few and they are very strictly observed, in like manner I thought that instead of the great many precepts of which logic is composed, I would have enough —if I made a firm and constant resolution not once to fail in the observation of them—in these four following:

The first was never to take anything for true except what I obviously knew to be so: that is to say, carefully to avoid hastiness and prejudgment and to admit nothing more in my judgment than what should so clearly and distinctly present itself to my mind that I could have no occasion to doubt it.

The second, to divide every one of the difficulties which I was to examine into as many small portions as were possible and necessary, the better to resolve them.

The third, to put my thoughts in order, beginning with the objects which are simplest and easiest to know, in order to rise little by little, as by degrees, up to the knowledge of the most complex, even imposing an order upon those which did not naturally fall into one.

And the last, to make everywhere such full enumerations and such general reviews that I might be confident to have omitted nothing.

Those long chains of reasoning (though simple and easy) which geometers commonly use to lead us to their most difficult demonstrations gave me occasion to imagine that all things which man can know follow one another in the same manner, and that, provided only that we abstain from receiving any one for true which is not and keep to the right order of deducing them one from another, there can be none so remote that we shall not at last come to it, nor so concealed that we shall not discover. I was not much troubled to inquire where I needed to begin, for I already knew that it was by the things which are simplest and easiest to know, and considering that among all those who have previously sought truth in the sciences, the mathematicians alone could find any demonstrations (that is to say, any certain and evident reasons) I did not doubt that it was by the same methods that they have carried out their investigations. (However I hoped for no other profit from them than to accustom my mind to nourish itself with truths, and not content itself with false reasons.) But for all this, I had no intention of trying to learn all those particular sciences which we commonly call mathematics; and, perceiving that although their objects are different, they nevertheless agree in considering nothing but the different ratios or proportions which are found among those objects, I thought it would be better to examine those proportions in general, without supposing them to be in those subjects which would make it easiest for me to know them (without, however, in any way limiting them, so that I might afterwards the better apply them to all other things where they might be appropriate.) . . .

I venture to say that the exact observation of those few precepts that I had chosen gave me such facility in resolving all the questions to which [algebra and geometry] give rise that in the two or three months which I employed in examining them, having begun by the most simple and most general and using every truth which I found as a rule which served to discover others, I not only arrived at several which I had formerly judged to be very difficult, but also it seemed to me near the end of my study that I could determine, even in those of which I was ignorant, by what means and to what extent it was possible to resolve them. In this perhaps I shall not appear to be too vain, if you consider that, as there is but one truth to everything, whoever finds it knows as much of it as one can know; and that, for example, a child instructed in arithmetic, having added some numbers according to the rules, can be sure to have found out concerning the sum that he examined all that the human intellect can discover. For, in a word, the method which teaches us to follow the true order and exactly to enumerate all the circumstances of what we seek contains everything that gives certainty to the rules of arithmetic.

But what pleased me most in this method was the assurance I had in using my reason in everything—if not perfectly, at least as best I could. Besides this I felt that in practicing it my mind little by little accustomed itself to conceive its objects more clearly and distinctly; and not having subjected it to any particular matter, I promised myself to apply it as profitably to the difficulties of other sciences as I had to algebra. Not that I therefore dared at first to undertake to examine everything which might present itself; for that would even have been contrary to the order which it prescribes. But, having become aware that all their principles had to be borrowed from philosophy, in which I had not yet found any that were certain, I thought it necessary for me in the first place to try to establish some. This being the most important thing in the world, and one where hastiness and prejudgment were most to be feared, I knew I ought not to undertake it until I attained a riper age (I was only twenty-three), and not before I had in the meantime employed a long time in preparing myself for this by rooting out of my mind all the wrong opinions I had before that time received, getting a stock of experience to serve afterward for the subject of my reasonings, and finally exercising myself always in the method which I had prescribed so that I might more and more strengthen myself in it.

Some Rules of Morality Drawn from the Method

From *Discourse on Method*, Part III.

Since it is not sufficient, before we begin to rebuild the house where we dwell, to pull it down and to make provision for materials and architects (or act as architects ourselves), or even to have carefully laid out the design of the new one, since we must also be provided with some other place to live conveniently during the time of the rebuilding, I formed for my use a provisional code of morality so that I might not remain irresolute in my actions during the time that reason obliged me to be so in my judgments and so that I might continue to live as happily as I could. This provisional morality consisted of only three or four maxims which I shall impart to you.

The first was to obey the laws and customs of my country, adhering steadfastly to that religion wherein by the grace of God I had from my infancy been brought up and in all other things behaving myself according to the least extreme and most moderate opinions which were commonly received in practice by the most judicious men among whom I was to live. For, beginning from that time to reckon my own opinions as nothing (since I wished to bring them all to the test), I was confident that I could not do better than follow

those of the most judicious. Although there are perhaps men as judicious among the Persians or Chinese as among us, yet it seemed to
me more fitting to regulate myself by those with whom I was to live.
And, so that I might know what really were their opinions, I tried
to observe what they practiced rather than what they said—not only
because, owing to the corruption of our morals, there are few men
who will say all that they believe, but also because several are themselves ignorant of their own beliefs. (Since the act of thought by
which we believe something is different from the one whereby we
know that we believe it, one often exists without the other.) Furthermore, among several opinions equally received, I chose the most
moderate only, both because they are always the most fit for practice
and probably also the best, all excess usually being wrong. Besides,
I would stray less from the right road if I should happen to err than
if, having chosen one of the extremes, it turned out to be other
which I should have followed. . . .

My second maxim was to be as constant and resolute in my actions
as I could and to follow with no less perseverance the most doubtful
opinions, when I had once determined them, than if they had been
most certain. In this I imitate travelers who, having lost their way
in a forest, ought not to wander, turning now this way and now that,
and still less to remain in one place; but should always advance as
straight as they can in one direction, nor change for some slight reason, even though perhaps at first it was only chance which determined them to choose it. For in this way, even if they do not go
directly where they wish, they will at least finally arrive somewhere
where they will probably be better off than in the middle of a forest.
So, the actions of this life often allowing no delay, it is a most certain
truth that when it is not in our power to discern the truest opinions,
we ought to follow the most probable; and even, when we can find
no more probability in one than the other, decide on some nevertheless, and afterwards no longer consider them as doubtful insofar
as they relate to practice, but as most true and certain, forasmuch as
the reason was so which made us determine them. . . .

My third maxim was to endeavor always rather to conquer myself
than Fortune; to change my desires rather than the order of the
world; and generally to accustom myself to believe that there is
nothing wholly in our power but our thoughts, so that after we have
done our best concerning things which are external to us, the things
wherein we fail should be taken to be absolutely impossible for us.
And this alone seemed to be sufficient to prevent me from desiring
in the future anything which I could not acquire and thus to render
me contented. For since our will naturally moves us to desire noth-

ing but those things which our understanding represents in some way as possible, it is certain that if we consider all the goods which are outside us as equally beyond our power, we shall have no more regret for the lack of those which seems to be due to our birth, when we are deprived of them through no fault of our own, than we have in not having possession of the realms of China or Mexico. Thus making (as we say) a virtue of necessity, we should no more desire to be in health if we are sick, or free if in prison, than we now do to have bodies of matter as incorruptible as diamonds or to have wings to fly like birds. But I admit that a long exercise and an often reiterated meditation is needed to accustom us to look on all things from this point of view. . . .

Finally, to conclude this code of morals, I thought fit to make a review of the various occupations which men have in this life, so that I might endeavor to choose the best. And without saying anything against any other man's, I thought I could do no better than continue in the same one wherein I was: that is, to employ all my life in cultivating my reason and to advance myself as far as I could in the knowledge of truth, following the method which I had prescribed for myself. I had proved to be so extremely contented since I began to use this method that I believed that no one in this life could be capable of any more sweet and innocent occupation; and daily discovering by means of it some truths which seemed to me of some importance, and which commonly other men were ignorant of, the satisfaction which I thereby received possessed my mind so much that other things did not concern me. Besides, the three preceding maxims were grounded only on the design which I had to continue to instruct myself. For God having given to each of us some light to discern the true from the false, I could not believe that I ought to content myself for one moment with the opinions of others unless I had proposed to myself to employ my judgment in due course in the examination of them; neither could I have felt free of scruples in following them had I not hoped to lose no opportunity to find out better ones, if there were any. . . .

After I was thus assured of these maxims and took them to heart along with the truths of the faith (which have always had first place in my mind) I judged that I might freely undertake to expel all the rest of my opinions. And inasmuch as I hoped to bring this to pass better by conversing with men rather than by remaining any longer in the stove where I had had all these thoughts, I returned to my travels before the winter was fully over. And in all the nine years following I did nothing but roll here and there about the world, trying to be a spectator rather than an actor in all the comedies which are acted therein, and reflecting particularly with regard to every subject on what might make it suspect or afford any occasion for mistake. In the meantime I rooted out of my mind all those errors which had formerly crept in. Not that I therein imitated the Skeptics, who doubt only for the sake of doubting and affect always to be undecided; for, on the contrary, all my design tended only to assure myself and to reject sands and quicksand in order to find rock and clay. It seemed to me that this succeeded well enough, in that in seeking to discover the falsehood or uncertainty of those propositions I examined—not by weak conjectures, but by clear and certain reasoning—I met with none so doubtful that I could not draw from them some conclusion which was certain enough, even if it were only that it contained nothing which was certain. And, as when pulling down an old house we usually keep the rubble to use in building the new one, so in destroying all those of my opinions which I judged ill-founded, I made various observations and acquired several experiences which have served me since to establish more certain ones. . . .

The Cogito *and the Proof of the* Existence *of God*

From *Discourse on Method*, Part IV.

I do not know if I ought to talk with you about the first meditations which I made on [the proofs of the existence of God], for they are so metaphysical and abstruse that perhaps they will not be to everyone's taste. However, so that you can judge if the foundations which I have laid are sufficiently solid, I find myself in some ways forced to speak of them. I had a long time ago observed that it is sometimes useful to follow opinions about morality which are very uncertain just as if they were incontestable (as I have stated earlier); but I did this in order to devote myself entirely to the search for truth, in which I thought it necessary to do just the opposite: to reject as absolutely false anything about which I could imagine the slightest doubt, in order to see if after all that there remained in my belief anything which was entirely indubitable. Hence, because our senses sometimes mislead us, I wished to suppose that there was nothing which was really as they make us imagine it. And because there are men who make mistakes in reasoning and fall into fallacies, even in the most simple questions of geometry, I, thinking myself just as fallible as the next man, rejected as false all reasons which I had previously taken for demonstrations. And finally, considering that we can have while we are asleep all of the same thoughts that we have when awake, with no idea when any of them are true, I hit upon the hypothesis that all the things which had ever entered my mind were no more true than the illusions of my dreams. But, immediately afterwards, I became aware that while I thus wished to think that everything was false, I who thought so must necessarily be something. And observing that this truth, *I think, therefore I am,* was so firm and certain that all the most extravagant suppositions of the skeptics were not capable of shaking it, I judged that I could receive it without hesitation as the first principle of the philosophy which I was seeking.

Then, examining what it was that I was, I saw that I could imagine that I did not have a body and that there was no world or other place where I was located; but I could not imagine withal that I did not exist. And, on the contrary, from the very fact that I could conceive doubts about the truth of other things it very obviously and certainly follows that I exist; and on the other hand, if I had only ceased to think, even if all the rest which I had imagined had been true, I would have had no reason to believe that I had existed. From this I knew that I was a substance of which the whole essence or nature was only to think; and which required for its existence no location in space, nor depended on any material thing. In this fashion I established that the self, that is to say the soul through which I am what I am, is entirely distinct from the body, and even that it is easier to know than the body; and that even if the body did not exist, the soul would nevertheless not cease to be what it is.

After this I considered in general the conditions for truth and certainty of a proposition; for since I had just discovered one which I knew to be so, I thought that I ought also to know in what this certainty consisted. And having observed that there is nothing in the proposition *I think, therefore I am* which assures me of its truth except that I see very clearly that in order to think it is necessary to exist, I judged that I could formulate a general rule that the things which we could conceive very clearly and very distinctly are wholly true, but that there remains only some difficulty in determining which ones we do conceive distinctly.

Following that, and reflecting on the fact that I doubted and that consequently my existence was not wholly perfect (for I saw clearly that it was a greater perfection to know than to doubt) I decided to

inquire from whence I had learned to think of something more perfect than I was; and I realized that obviously this must be from
some nature which was in fact more perfect. As for those thoughts
which I had of several other things outside myself, such as the heavens, the earth, light, heat, and a thousand others, I had no trouble
in knowing their origin, because, not observing anything in them
which seemed to make them superior to me, I was able to believe
that if they were true, they were true in virtue of their dependence
upon my nature (insofar as it had any perfection); and if they were
not true, that I held them from nothing—that is, that they were in
me in consequence of some defect which I had. But this could not
be true of the idea of a being more perfect than mine; for to reach
it from nothing would be manifestly impossible. And since it is
equally repugnant to reason that the perfect could depend upon or
follow from the less perfect—since this would be for something to
come from nothing—I could not have arrived at it by myself. Thus
the only remaining explanation is that it was placed in me by a nature which was truly more perfect than I was; furthermore that it
had within itself all the perfections of which I could have any idea
—in a word, that it was God. To this I shall add that since I knew
some perfections which I did not have, I was not the only being
which exists . . . but that it followed of necessity that there must
be some other more perfect being, on which I depended and from
which I had acquired everything that I have. For, if I had been alone
and independent of any other thing, so that I should have had from
myself everything of that little perfection of being in which I par-
ticipated, I should have had from myself, by the same reasoning, all
the rest of it which I was conscious of lacking, and thus would myself have been infinite, eternal, unchangeable, omniscient, omnipotent, and, in short, would have had all the perfections which I could
observe in God. For it follows from the reasonings which I have just
made that in order to know the nature of God (as much of it as my
nature was capable of knowing) I had only to consider with respect
to everything of which I found some idea in myself whether or not
it was a perfection to possess them: and I was certain that none of
those which gave evidence of some imperfection were in him,
whereas all the others were. Thus I saw that doubt, inconstancy,
sadness, and such things could not be in him, since I would have
been glad to be exempt from them myself. Then, beyond this, I had
ideas of many corporeal and perceptible things; for, although I
might suppose that I was dreaming and that all which I saw or imagined was false, I nevertheless could not deny that the ideas were
truly in my mind. But because I had already very clearly established

in my mind that the nature of intelligence is distinct from physical nature, and considering that all admixture is evidence of dependency, and that dependency is obviously a defect, I concluded from this that it could not be a perfection in God to be composed of a mixture of these two natures, and that consequently he was not so composed. But I concluded that if there were any bodies in the world, or else some intelligences and other entities which were not entirely perfect, their existence must depend on his power to such a degree that without him they could not endure for an instant.

After that I desired to search for other truths. The object of geometers presented itself to me, which I conceived to be like a continuous body, or a space indefinitely extended in length, width, and height or depth, divisible into various parts which could have various shapes and sizes and which could be changed or transposed in all kinds of ways (for the geometers suppose all of this in the object of their study); so I ran through several of their most simple demonstrations. And having become aware that the great certainty that everyone attributes to these demonstrations is founded only on the fact that they are clearly conceived (following the rule which I have just now spoken of), I also become aware that there is nothing at all in their demonstrations to assure me of the existence of their object. For example, I easily saw that in any given triangle, the sum of the three angles would be equal to two right angles; but I did not see in that anything which assured me that there was any actual triangle in the world. But on the other hand, returning to the idea that I had of a perfect Being, I found that existence was included in it in the same way that it is included in the idea of a triangle that its three angles are equal to two right angles, or in that of a circle that all points on its circumference are equally distant from the center; or even more obviously than these. Consequently it is at least as certain that God, who is the perfect Being, is, or exists, as any demonstration of geometry can be.

But that which causes many to persuade themselves that there is difficulty in knowing this truth, and even also in knowing the nature of their souls, is that their minds never transcend the objects of the senses and that they are so accustomed to considering nothing except by imagining it (which is a fashion of thought especially suitable for material objects) that anything which is unimaginable seems to them unintelligible. This is sufficiently evident from the fact that even the scholastic philosophers hold to the maxim that there is nothing in the understanding which was not first in the senses— where, however, there is no doubt that the ideas of God and of the soul have never been. And it seems to me that those who wish to use their imaginations to understand these ideas act in just the same way as if they wanted to use their eyes in order to hear sounds or smell odors—with this further difference, that the sense of vision gives us as much assurance of the truth of its objects as do those of smell or hearing, whereas neither our imagination nor our senses can ever provide certainty of anything without the intervention of our understanding.

Finally, if there are still men who are not sufficiently convinced of the existence of God and of their souls by the reasons which I have adduced, I wish them to know that all other things of which perhaps they think themselves more certain, such as having a body, that there are stars and an earth, and such things, are less certain. For though we have a moral assurance of these things which is such that it would be extravagant, to say the least, for us to doubt them; yet nevertheless no one can reasonably deny, from the identical awareness we may have in dreams that we have a body and, see other stars and another earth, without there being any such things, that when it comes to a question of metaphysical certainty there is not enough in these matters for us to be wholly convinced of them. For how do we know that the thoughts which come to us in dreams are false rather than the others, since they are often just as vivid and specific? Let the best minds study the question as much as they please, I do not believe they can give any reason sufficient to remove the doubt unless they presuppose the existence of God. For, in the first place, that which I have just laid down as a rule—that is, that the things which we conceive very clearly and very distinctly are all true—is certain only because God is or exists, is a perfect being, and because all that it is in us comes from him. From this it follows that our ideas or notions, in that they are real things which come from God, cannot fail to be true to the extent that they are clear and distinct. Furthermore, although we quite often have ideas which contain some falsity, this can only be because they contain something confused or obscure—in this respect participating in nothingness (that is to say, they are only confused in this way in us because we are not entirely perfect). And it is evident that the idea that truth or perfection can proceed from nothingness is just as repugnant as the idea that falsity or imperfection can proceed from God. But if we did not know that all of the real and the true that is in us comes from a perfect and infinite being, no matter how clear and distinct our ideas were, we would have no grounds of assurance that they had the perfection of being true.

Now after the knowledge of the soul and of God has made us certain of this rule, it is easy to know that the dreams of our imaginations while we are asleep can provide no reason to doubt the truth of the thoughts which we have while awake. For even if it should happen that we should have some very distinct idea while asleep, as for example that a geometer invents some new demonstration, the fact that he was asleep does not keep it from being true. And as to the most common error in our dreams, which is that they represent various objects to us in the same way that our external senses do, it does not matter that this gives occasion for us to suspect the truth of such ideas, because the senses can deceive us often enough without our being asleep—as when those with jaundice see everything as colored yellow or when the stars and other very remote objects appear to us as much smaller than they really are. For, in short, whether we wake or sleep we ought never to allow ourselves to be persuaded of anything except on the evidence of our reason. It should be observed that I speak of our reason and not of our imagination nor of our senses; just as we ought not to judge that the sun is really the size that it appears to be, even though we see it very clearly, and as we can well imagine distinctly the head of a lion grafted on the body of a goat without necessarily concluding from this that there is such a thing in the world as a chimera. For reason does not dictate that everything which we thus see or imagine is true; but it does tell us clearly that all our ideas or notions ought to have some foundation in truth, since otherwise it could not be possible that God, who is entirely perfect and truthful, could have placed them in us. And because our reasonings during sleep are never so evident or so complete as those while we are awake, although sometimes our imagination then might be even more explicit and vivid, reason tells us also that since our thoughts can not possibly be all true, because we are not entirely perfect, that which they have of truth must infallibly be met in those we have while awake rather than in our dreams.

Our Knowledge of the Physical World and of Ourselves

From Descartes, *Meditations* (Paris, 1641), II. Translated from the French edition of 1647.

Let us begin by considering the most common things, things which we believe we understand most distinctly: that is, bodies which we touch and see. I do not mean to speak of bodies in general, for these general concepts are usually more confused, but let us consider some particular body. Let us take, for example, this bit of wax which has just been taken from the hive. It has not yet lost the sweetness of the honey which it holds; it still retains something of the fragrance of the flowers from which it has been composed. Its color, shape, and size are apparent; it is hard, it is cold, we can handle it, and if you strike it, it gives out a certain sound. In a word, all the things which can make us distinctly recognize a body are present in this one.

But now suppose that while I speak thus, someone brings the wax close to the fire. The remnants of its taste evaporate; the fragrance vanishes, its color changes, it loses its shape, and its size increases. It becomes liquid and so hot that one can scarcely touch it; when we strike it, it emits no sound. Does the same wax remain, after all these changes? Of course we must admit that it does; no one would deny it. What is it, then, that we know with so much clarity in this bit of wax? Certainly it could not be anything that I notice through the intermediary of the senses, since everything that falls under taste, smell, sight, touch, or hearing is found to be changed, and yet the same wax remains. Perhaps it was what I now think, namely that the wax was neither this sweetness of honey, nor this pleasant scent of flowers, nor this whiteness, nor this shape, nor this sound, but only a body which previously appeared to me under these forms, and now presents itself under others. But, speaking precisely, what is it that I imagine when I conceive it in this fashion? Let us consider it attentively, abstracting all those things which do not belong to the wax, and see what remains. Certainly nothing is left but something extended, flexible, and subject to change. But what do we mean by "flexible" and "subject to change"? Is it that I imagine that this round piece of wax can become square, and from being square can be molded into a triangular shape? Certainly not. It cannot be that, since I conceive it as capable of undergoing an infinite number of such changes, an infinity beyond what I would ever know how to run through in my imagination; and thus the conception which I have of the wax is not gained by the faculty of imagination.

Now what is this quality of "extension"? Is it not equally unknown, since as the wax melts, it increases in size, being larger still when entirely melted, and a great deal larger as the heat increases still more? And I shall not attain to a clear and truthful conception of the wax if I do not consider that it is capable of more varieties of extension than I have ever imagined. Thus I am forced to the conclusion that I could never reach through the imagination any conception of the wax and that it is only my understanding which conceives it—I say, conceives this particular bit of wax, since it is even more evident that only the understanding can conceive of wax in general. Now what is this wax which can only be conceived by the understanding or the mind? Certainly it is the same which I see, touch, and imagine, and the same which I knew from the beginning. But what must be particularly noticed is that the perception of it— or better, the action by which we perceive it—is not seeing, nor touching, nor imagining, and never has been (though it formerly seemed to be) but only an inspection of the mind, which may be imperfect and confused, as it was formerly, or clear and distinct, as it is at present, depending on how my attention is more or less directed to the things which are in it and of which it is composed.

However, I am thoroughly astonished when I consider how weak my mind is and how inclined it is to slip unnoticed into error. For even when I try to think things over by myself without speaking, words interrupt me, and I am almost deceived by the terms of ordinary language. For example, we say that we see the same wax, if someone shows it to us, rather than that we judge that it is the same in that it has the same color and same shape. From this I would almost conclude that we know the wax by the vision of our eyes rather than entirely by the inspection of the mind, if by chance I had not looked out the window at the men passing in the street. The sight of them makes me say that I see men, in the same way that I say I see the wax; but what do I see through the window, in fact, but hats and cloaks, which could cover ghosts or robots? Yet I judge these to be real men, and thus solely by the power of judgment that resides in my mind I understand what I believed I saw with my eyes.

A man who attempts to elevate his knowledge above the ordinary ought to be ashamed to take his occasions for doubting from the forms of speech employed by the vulgar. I prefer to pass on, and consider whether I had a more evident and perfect conception of what the wax was when I first perceived it and believed that I knew it by means of the external senses or by so-called common sense (that is, by the power of imagination), or whether I conceive it better at present, after having more exactly examined what it is and in what manner it can be known. Certainly it would be ridiculous to claim that the latter is not the case; for what was there in the first perception which was distinct and evident, or which could not be apprehended in just the same way by the senses of the lowest animal? But when I distinguish the wax from its external forms, it is as if I had stripped off its vestments and consider it entirely naked.

Certainly, although some error may still be found in my judgment, I nevertheless cannot conceive it in this way without a human mind. But finally what shall I say of this mind—that is to say, of myself? (For up to here I do not admit in myself anything other than a mind.) What shall I declare about myself, who seem to conceive with so much clarity and distinctness this piece of wax? Do I not know myself not only with more certainty and truth, but also with still more clarity and distinctness? For if I judge that the wax is or exists in that I see it, certainly it follows even more evidently that I am, that I myself exist, in that I see it. For it could be that what I see is not in fact wax; it could even happen that I do not have eyes to see anything; but it cannot possibly be true that when I see, or—and I make no distinction here—when I think that I see, the "I" which thinks is not something. . . .

Now if the idea or the knowledge of the wax seems to be more clear and distinct after it has been discovered not only by sight or by touch but by many other causes as well, with how much more evidence, clarity, and distinctness ought I to know myself, since all the reasons which serve to know and conceive the nature of the wax or some other body prove much more easily and evidently the nature of my mind?

Part IV

LOCKE AND THE FOUNDATIONS OF EMPIRICISM

Introduction

Especially in philosophers, style is the man. The brilliance of Hobbes and the brisk assurance of Descartes suit their conviction that at last the right mind has been married to the right method. Writers of a more empirical turn, wishing to look for truth in the great world rather than in the narrow cells of human wit, characteristically develop their thought in a more modest and tentative way. These characteristics are particularly noticeable in the book which might be described as the foundation of British empiricism, John Locke's *Essay Concerning Human Understanding*.

Certainly the *Essay* does not suffer from overly rigid organization. As Locke tells us in the introduction, it was born out of the difficulties that arose in a discussion among five or six friends in Locke's rooms. Locke suggested that before they tackle more adventurous questions, they ought to consider what the human understanding is capable of comprehending, and so they agreed to meet next to discuss the intellect as an instrument. Locke jotted down a few notes (he says that at first he thought he could put down everything worth saying on a single sheet of paper) and the discussion was duly held. But that was not the end of the matter; as Locke relates, "the farther I went, the larger prospect I had; new discoveries led me still on and so it grew insensibly to the bulk it now appears in." This Topsy of philosophical literature now has a bulk of 700 pages or so, and a sense of form aptly conveyed by its author's account of its genesis: "begun by chance, continued by intreaty, written by incoherent parcels, and after long intervals of neglect resumed again as my humor or occasions permitted."

This *Essay* thus sprawled into almost every area of philosophy. We can give only a sample of the arguments against innate ideas, but it is important to remember that other parts of the essay, though difficult to summarize or convey in any introductory form, are nonetheless of great importance. Locke's work generally, like his destruction of innate ideas, is of most value for what it refutes. This again is just as he said:

> The commonwealth of learning is not at this time without master-builders whose mighty designs in advancing the sciences will leave lasting monuments to the admiration of posterity. But everyone must not hope to be a Boyle or a Sydenham, and in an age that produces such masters as the great Huygenius and the incomparable Mr. Newton, with some others of that strain, 'tis ambition enough to be employed as an under-laborer in clearing the ground a little and removing some of the rubbish that lies in the way to knowledge.

The chief species of rubbish, Locke thought, was the "learned but frivolous use of uncouth, affected, or unintelligible terms," and he made it his particular labor to attack such examples as the scholastic concept of "substance," which he showed, by an excellent piece of language analysis, to be entirely superfluous.

It is true that Locke is seldom very careful to specify the origins of the rubbish which he desires to cart away. He lacked that excellent philosophical habit of stating the arguments he was to confute in their most refined and powerful form, and much learned ingenuity has been spent on identifying the original form and configuration of the arguments which he attacks. It appears that the sermons and pamphlets of various country parsons which Locke had encountered, rather than the theories of Descartes and the Cambridge Platonists, formulated the doctrines which Locke was to oppose. For the explanation of this circumstance, we may look to Locke's unsystematic (though wide) reading and his habit of becoming entangled in polemical pamphleteering. He would doubtless have been a better philosopher had he mastered the best of Descartes or Henry More on innate ideas; but this shortcoming is irrelevant to any discussion of his historical position.

Furthermore, Locke's philosophy has more than a negative importance. It was no small achievement to take up the hint that epistemology should be the central theme of philosophy and to develop it at such length, and the impact of Locke's works in the eighteenth century shows that the encumbrances from which he delivered men's minds were not imaginary ones. His interest in language was likewise novel and suggestive, and indeed it is the best example of the seminal potency of his thought. Muddled and untidy as it often was, it contained dozens of ideas that later philosophers could investigate and later men live by. (Hume's development of Locke's ideas on causation is as good an example as Jefferson's application of his ideas on politics.) The dream of the great rationalists, after all, was to put an end to philosophy by solving all its problems. That was not Locke's hope; he preferred to keep philosophy close to life, with all its "buzzing blooming confusion," rather than take the path of drastic abstraction.

The Limits of Understanding

From John Locke, *Essay Concerning Human Understanding,* 4th ed. (London, 1700), Book I, chap. i.

1. Since it is the understanding that sets man above the rest of sensible beings and gives him all the advantage and dominion which he has over them, it is certainly a subject, even for its nobleness, worth our labor to inquire into. The understanding, like the eye, whilst it makes us see and perceive all other things, takes no notice of itself; and it requires art and pains to set it at a distance and make it its own object. But whatever be the difficulties that lie in the way of this inquiry, whatever it be that keeps us so much in the dark to ourselves, sure I am that all the light we can let in upon our own minds, all the acquaintance we can make with our own understandings, will not only be very pleasant, but bring us great advantage in directing our thoughts in the search of other things.

2. This, therefore, being my purpose—to inquire into the original, certainty, and extent of human knowledge, together with the grounds and degrees of belief, opinion, and assent—I shall not at present meddle with the physical consideration of the mind, or trouble myself to examine wherein its essence consists, or by what motions of our spirits or alterations of our bodies we come to have any sensation by our organs, or any ideas in our understandings; and whether those ideas do in their formation (any or all of them) depend on matter or no. These are speculations which, however curious and entertaining, I shall decline, as lying out of my way in

the design I am now upon. It shall suffice to my present purpose to consider the discerning faculties of a man, as they are employed about the objects which they have to do with. And I shall imagine I have not wholly misemployed myself in the thoughts I shall have on this occasion if, in this historical, plain method I can give any account of the ways whereby our understandings come to attain those notions of things we have and can set down any measures of the certainty of our knowledge, or the grounds of those persuasions which are to be found amongst men, so various, different, and wholly contradictory; and yet asserted somewhere or other with such assurance and confidence that he that shall take a view of the opinions of mankind, observe their opposition, and at the same time consider the fondness and devotion wherewith they are embraced, the resolution and eagerness wherewith they are maintained, may perhaps have reason to suspect that either there is no such thing as truth at all, or that mankind hath no sufficient means to attain a certain knowledge of it.

3. It is therefore worthwhile to search out the bounds between opinion and knowledge and examine by what measures, in things whereof we have no certain knowledge, we ought to regulate our assent and moderate our persuasion. In order whereunto I shall pursue this following method:

First, I shall inquire into the original of those ideas, notions, or whatever else you please to call them, which a man observes and is conscious to himself he has in his mind, and the ways whereby the understanding comes to be furnished with them.

Secondly, I shall endeavor to show what knowledge the understanding hath by those ideas, and the certainty, evidence, and extent of it.

Thirdly, I shall make some inquiry into the nature and grounds of faith or opinion: whereby I mean that assent which we give to any proposition as true, of whose truth yet we have no certain knowledge. And here we shall have occasion to examine the reasons and degrees of assent.

4. If by this inquiry into the nature of the understanding I can discover the powers thereof, how far they reach, to what things they are in any degree proportionate, and where they fail us, I suppose it may be of use to prevail with the busy mind of man to be more cautious in meddling with things exceeding its comprehension; to stop when it is at the utmost extent of its tether; and to sit down in a quiet ignorance of those things which, upon examination, are found to be beyond the reach of our capacities. We should not then perhaps be so forward, out of an affectation of an universal knowl-

edge, to raise questions and perplex ourselves and others with disputes about things to which our understandings are not suited, and
of which we cannot frame in our minds any clear or distinct perceptions, or whereof (as it has perhaps too often happened) we have not
any notions at all. If we can find out how far the understanding can
extend its view, how far it has faculties to attain certainty, and in
what cases it can only judge and guess, we may learn to content ourselves with what is attainable by us in this state.

5. For though the comprehension of our understandings comes exceeding short of the vast extent of things, yet we shall have cause
enough to magnify the bountiful Author of our being for that proportion and degree of knowledge he has bestowed on us, so far
above all the rest of the inhabitants of this our mansion. Men have
reason to be well satisfied with what God hath thought fit for them.
. . . How short soever their knowledge may come of an universal
or perfect comprehension of whatsoever is, it yet secures their great
concernments that they have light enough to lead them to the knowledge of their Maker and the sight of their own duties. . . . We shall
not have much reason to complain of the narrowness of our minds
if we will but employ them about what may be of use to us; for of
that they are very capable. And it will be an unpardonable as well
as childish peevishness if we undervalue the advantages of our
knowledge and neglect to improve it to the ends for which it was
given us because there are some things that are set out of the reach
of it. It will be no excuse to an idle and untoward servant who
would not attend his business by candle light to plead that he had
not broad sunshine. The Candle that is set up in us shines bright
enough for all our purposes. The discoveries we can make with this
ought to satisfy us; and we shall then use our understandings right
when we entertain all objects in that way and proportion that they
are suited to our faculties (and upon those grounds they are capable
of being proposed to us); and not peremptorily or intemperately
require demonstration and demand certainty where probability only
is to be had. . . .

8. . . . Before I proceed on to what I have thought on this subject
I must here in the entrance beg pardon of my reader for the frequent
use of the word "idea" which he will find in the following treatise.
It being that term which, I think, serves best to stand for whatsoever
is the object of the understanding when a man thinks, I have used
it to express whatever is meant by phantasm, notion, species, or
whatever it is which the mind can be employed about in thinking;
and I could not avoid frequently using it.

I presume it will be easily granted me that there are such ideas in men's minds; everyone is conscious of them in himself, and men's words and actions will satisfy him that they are in others.

Our first inquiry then shall be: how they come into the mind.

No Innate Speculative Principles

From *Essay on Human Understanding*, 4th ed., Book I, chap. ii.

1. It is an established opinion amongst some men that there are in the understanding certain innate principles: some primary notions, κοιναὶ ἔννοιαι characters, as it were stamped upon the mind of man, which the soul receives in its very first being and brings into the world with it. It would be sufficient to convince unprejudiced readers of the falseness of this supposition if I should only show (as I hope I shall in the following parts of this discourse) how men, barely by the use of their natural faculties, may attain to all the knowledge they have without the help of any innate impressions, and may arrive at certainty without any such original notions or principles. For I imagine anyone will easily grant that it would be impertinent to suppose the ideas of colors innate in a creature to whom God hath given sight and a power to receive them by the eyes from external objects; and no less unreasonable would it be to attribute several truths to the impressions of nature and innate characters, when we may observe in ourselves faculties fit to attain as easy and certain knowledge of them as if they were originally imprinted on the mind.

But because a man is not permitted without censure to follow his own thoughts in the search of truth, when they lead him ever so little out of the common road, I shall set down the reasons that made me doubt of the truth of that opinion as an excuse for my mistake, if I be in one—which I leave to be considered by those who, with me, dispose themselves to embrace truth wherever they find it.

2. There is nothing more commonly taken for granted than that there are certain principles both speculative and practical (for they speak of both) universally agreed upon by all mankind: which therefore they argue must needs be the constant impressions which the souls of men receive in their first beings, and which they bring into the world with them as necessarily and really as they do any of their inherent faculties.

3. This argument, drawn from universal consent, has this misfortune

in it, that if it were true in matter of fact that there were certain truths wherein all mankind agreed, it would not prove them innate if there can be any other way shown how men may come to that universal agreement in the things they do consent in; which I presume may be done.

4. But, which is worse, this argument of universal consent, which is made use of to prove innate principles, seems to me a demonstration that there are none such: because there are none to which all mankind give an universal assent. I shall begin with the speculative, and instance in those magnified principles of demonstration, 'Whatsoever is, is,' and 'It is impossible for the same thing to be and not to be'; which of all others, I think, have the most allowed title to innate . . . have so settled a reputation of maxims universally received, that it will no doubt be thought strange if anyone should seem to question it. But yet I take liberty to say that these propositions are so far from having an universal assent that there are a great part of mankind to whom they are not so much as known.

5. For, first, it is evident that all children and idiots have not the least apprehension or thought of them; and the want of that is enough to destroy that universal assent which must needs be the necessary concomitant of all innate truths, it seeming to me near a contradiction to say that there are truths imprinted on the soul which it perceives or understands not (imprinting, if it signify anything, being nothing else but the making certain truths to be perceived). For to imprint anything on the mind without the mind's perceiving it seems to me hardly intelligible. If therefore children and idiots have souls, have minds, with those impressions upon them, they must unavoidably perceive them and necessarily know and assent to these truths; which since they do not, it is evident that there are no such impressions. . . .

6. To avoid this, it is usually answered that all men know and assent to them when they come to the use of reason, and this is enough to prove them innate. I answer:

7. Doubtful expressions that have scarce any signification go for clear reasons to those who, being prepossessed, take not the pains to examine even what they themselves say. For to apply this answer with any tolerable sense to our present purpose, it must signify one of these two things: either that as soon as men come to the use of reason these supposed native inscriptions come to be known and observed by them; or else, that the use and exercise of men's reason assists them in the discovery of these principles, and certainly makes them known to them.

8. If they mean that by the use of reason men may discover these principles, and that this is sufficient to prove them innate; their way of arguing will stand thus: viz., that whatever truths reason can certainly discover to us and make us firmly assent to, those are all naturally imprinted on the mind; since that universal assent which is made the mark of them, amounts to no more than this—that by the use of reason we are capable to come to a certain knowledge of and assent to them; and by this means, there will be no difference between the maxims of the mathematicians and theorems they deduce from them; all must be equally allowed innate, they being all discoveries made by the use of reason, and truths that a rational creature may certainly come to know if he apply his thoughts rightly that way.

9. But how can these men think the use of reason necessary to discover principles that are supposed innate, when reason (if we may believe them) is nothing else but the faculty of deducing unknown truths from principles or propositions that are already known? That certainly can never be thought innate which we have need of reason to discover—unless, as I have said, we will have all the certain truths that reason ever teaches us to be innate. We may as well think the use of reason necessary to make our eyes discover visible objects as that there should be need of reason or the exercise thereof to make the understanding see what is originally engraven in it, and cannot be in the understanding before it be perceived by it. So that to make reason discover those truths thus imprinted is to say that the use of reason discovers to a man what he knew before; and if men have those innate impressed truths originally, and before the use of reason, and yet are always ignorant of them till they come to the use of reason, it is in effect to say that men know and know them not at the same time.

*   *   *

12. If by knowing and assenting to them 'when we come to the use of reason' be meant that this is the time when they come to be taken notice of by the mind, and that as soon as children come to the use of reason, they come also to know and assent to these maxims, this also is false and frivolous. First, it is false, because it is evident these maxims are not in the mind so early as the use of reason; and therefore the coming to the use of reason is falsely assigned as the time of their discovery. How many instances of the use of reason may we observe in children a long time before they have any knowledge of this maxim: "That it is impossible for the same thing to be and not to be?" And a great part of illiterate people and savages pass many

years, even of their rational age, without ever thinking on this and
the like general propositions. I grant men come not to the knowledge of these general and more abstract truths, which are thought
innate, till they come to the use of reason; and I add: nor then
neither. Which is so because till after they come to the use of reason
those general abstract ideas are not framed in the mind . . . but are
indeed discoveries made and verities introduced and brought into
the mind by the same way and discovered by the same steps as several
other propositions which nobody was ever so extravagant as to suppose innate. This I hope to make plain in the sequel of this Discourse. I allow therefore a necessity that men should come to the
use of reason before they get the knowledge of those general truths,
but deny that men's coming to the use of reason is the time of their
discovery.

*   *   *

14. But secondly, were it true that the precise time of their being
known and assented to were when men come to the use of reason,
neither would that prove them innate. This way of arguing is as
frivolous as the supposition of itself is false. For by what kind of
logic will it appear that any notion is originally by nature imprinted
in the mind in its first constitution because it comes first to be observed and assented to when a faculty of the mind which has quite
a distinct province begins to exert itself? And therefore the coming
to the use of speech, if it were supposed the time that these maxims
are first assented to (which it may be with as much truth, as the time
when men come to the use of reason) would be as good a proof that
they were innate as to say they are innate because men assent to
them when they come to the use of reason. . . . All that can with
any truth be meant by this proposition that men "assent to them
when they come to the use of reason" is no more but this: that the
making of general abstract ideas and the understanding of general
names being a concomitant of the rational faculty and growing up
with it, children commonly get not those general ideas nor learn the
names that stand for them till, having for a good while exercised
their reason about familiar and more particular ideas, they are by
their ordinary discourse and actions with others acknowledged to be
capable of rational conversation. . . .

15. The senses at first let in particular ideas and furnish the yet
empty cabinet; and the mind by degrees growing familiar with some
of them, they are lodged in the memory and names got to them.
Afterwards the mind proceeding farther abstracts them and by degrees learns the use of general names. In this manner the mind

comes to be furnished with ideas and language, the materials about which to exercise its discursive faculty; and the use of reason becomes daily more visible as these materials that give it employment increase. But though the having of general ideas and the use of general words and reason usually grow together, yet I see not how this any way proves them innate. The knowledge of some truths, I confess, is very early in the mind, but in a way that shows them not to be innate. For, if we will observe, we shall find it still to be about ideas not innate, but acquired; it being about those first which are imprinted by external things, with which infants have earliest to do, and which make the most frequent impressions on their senses. In ideas thus got, the mind discovers that some agree and others differ, probably as soon as it has any use of memory—as soon as it is able to retain and receive distinct ideas. But whether it be then or no, this is certain: it does so long before it has the use of words, or comes to that which we commonly call the use of reason. For a child knows as certainly before it can speak the difference between the ideas of sweet and bitter (i.e., that sweet is not bitter) as it knows afterwards (when it comes to speak) that wormwood and sugarplums are not the same thing.

*   *   *

24. To conclude this argument of universal consent, I agree with these defenders of innate principles that if they are innate, they must needs have universal assent. For that a truth should be innate and yet not assented to is to me as unintelligible as for a man to know a truth and be ignorant of it at the same time. But then, by these men's own confession, they cannot be innate, since they are not assented to by those who understand not the terms, nor by a great part of those who do understand them but have yet never heard nor thought of those propositions: which, I think, is at least one half of mankind. But were the number far less, it would be enough to destroy universal assent and thereby show these propositions not to be innate, if children alone were ignorant of them.

25. But that I may not be accused to argue from the thoughts of infants, which are unknown to us, and to conclude from what passes in their understandings before they express it, I say next that these two general propositions are not the truths that first possess the minds of children, nor are antecedent to all acquired and adventitious notions; which if they were innate they must needs be. Whether we can determine it or no, it matters not; there is certainly a time when children begin to think, and their words and actions do assure us that they do so. When therefore they are capable

of thought, of knowledge, of assent, can it rationally be supposed they can be ignorant of those notions that nature has imprinted, were there any such? . . . The child certainly knows that the nurse that feeds it is neither the cat it plays with nor the blackmore it is afraid of; that the wormseed or mustard it refuses is not the apple or sugar it cries for; this is certainly and undoubtedly assured of, but will anyone say it is by virtue of this principle, that it is impossible for the same thing to be and not to be, that it so firmly assents to these and other parts of its knowledge? Or that the child has any notion or apprehension of that proposition at an age wherein yet 'tis plain it knows a great many other truths? He that will say children join [in] these general abstract speculations with their sucking bottles and their rattles may perhaps with justice be thought to have more passion and zeal for his opinion, but less sincerity and truth, than one of that age.

26. Though therefore there be several general propositions that meet with constant and ready assent as soon as proposed to men grown up, who have attained the use of more general and abstract ideas and names standing for them, yet they not being to be found in those of tender years, who nevertheless know other things, they cannot pretend to universal assent of intelligent persons, and so by no means can be supposed innate, it being impossible that any truth which is innate (if there were any such) should be unknown, at least to anyone who knows anything else.

27. . . . These characters, if they were native and original impressions, should appear fairest and clearest in those persons in whom yet we find no footsteps of them; and 'tis, in my opinion, a strong presumption that they are not innate, since they are least known to those in whom, if they were innate, they must needs exert themselves with most force and vigor. For children, idiots, savages, and illiterate people, being of all others the least corrupted by custom or borrowed opinions—learning and education having not cast their native thoughts into new molds, nor by superinducing foreign and studied doctrines confounded those fair characters nature had written there—one might reasonably imagine that in their minds these innate notions should lie open fairly to everyone's view, as it is certain the thoughts of children do. . . . But alas, amongst children, idiots, savages, and the grossly illiterate, what general maxims are to be found? what universal principles of knowledge? Their notions are few and narrow, borrowed only from those objects they have had most to do with and which have made upon their senses the frequentest and strongest impressions. A child knows his nurse and his cradle, and by degrees the playthings of a little more ad-

vanced age; and a young savage has, perhaps, his head filled with love and hunting, according to the fashion of his tribe. But he that from a child untaught or a wild inhabitant of the woods will expect these abstract maxims and reputed principles of sciences will, I fear, find himself mistaken. . . . They are the language and business of the schools and academies of learned nations, accustomed to that sort of conversation or learning where disputes are frequent, these maxims being suited to artificial argumentation and useful for conviction, but not much conducing to the discovery of truth or advancement of knowledge.

No Innate Practical Principles

From *Essay Concerning Human Understanding*, 4th ed., Book I, chap. iii.

1. If those speculative maxims whereof we discoursed in the foregoing chapter have not an actual universal assent from all mankind, as we there proved, it is much more visible concerning practical principles that they come short of an universal reception; and I think it will be hard to instance any one moral rule which can pretend to so general and ready an assent as "What is, is," or to be so manifest a truth as this, "that it is impossible for the same thing to be and not to be." Whereby it is evident that they are farther removed from a title to be innate, and the doubt of their being native impressions on the mind is stronger against these moral principles than the other. Not that it brings their truth at all in question. They are equally true, though not equally evident. Those speculative maxims carry their own evidence with them; but moral principles require reasoning and discourse, and some exercise of the mind, to discover the certainty of their truth. They lie not open as natural characters engraven on the mind, which, if any such were, they must needs be visible by themselves, and by their own light be certain and known to everybody. . . .

2. Whether there be any such moral principles wherein all men do agree, I appeal to any who have been but moderately conversant in the history of mankind and looked abroad beyond the smoke of their own chimneys. Where is that practical truth that is universally received without doubt or question, as it must be if innate? Justice and keeping of contracts is that which most men seem to agree in.

This is a principle which is thought to extend itself to the dens of thieves. . . . I grant that outlaws themselves do this one amongst another: but 'tis without receiving these as the innate laws of nature. They practice them as rules of convenience within their own communities; but it is impossible to conceive that he embraces justice as a practical principle who acts fairly with his fellow-highwaymen and at the same time plunders or kills the next honest man he meets with. . . .

*   *   *

4. Another reason that makes me doubt of any innate practical principles is that I think there cannot any one moral rule be proposed whereof a man may not justly demand a reason: which would be perfectly ridiculous and absurd if they were innate. . . .

5. That men should keep their compacts is certainly a great and undeniable rule in morality. But yet if a Christian, who has the view of happiness and misery in another life, be asked why a man must keep his word, he will give this as a reason: because God, who has the power of eternal life and death, requires it of us. But if a Hobbist be asked why, he will answer: because the public requires it, and the Leviathan will punish you if you do not. And if one of the old heathen philosophers had been asked, he would have answered: because it was dishonest, below the dignity of a man, and opposite to virtue, the highest perfection of human nature, to do otherwise.

6. Hence naturally flows the great variety of opinions concerning moral rules which are to be found amongst men. . . .

*   *   *

9. I cannot see how any men should ever transgress those moral rules with confidence and serenity were they innate and stamped upon their minds. View but an army at the sacking of a town, and see what observation or sense of moral principles, or what touch of conscience, for all the outrages they do. Robberies, murders, rapes are the sports of men set at liberty from punishment and censure. Have there not been whole nations, and those of the most civilized people, amongst whom the exposing their children and leaving them in the fields to perish by want or wild beasts has been the practice, as little condemned or scrupled as the begetting them? . . . It is familiar amongst the Mengrelians, a people professing Christianity, to bury their children alive without scruple. There are places where they eat their own children. The Caribs were wont to geld their children, on purpose to fat and eat them. And Garcilasso de la Vega tells us of a people in Peru which were wont to fat and eat the

children they got on their female captives, whom they kept as concubines for that purpose; and when they were past breeding, the mothers themselves were killed too and eaten. . . .

The Origin of Our Ideas

From *Essay Concerning Human Understanding*, 4th ed., Book II, chap. i.

1. I know it is a received doctrine that men have native ideas and original characters stamped upon their minds in their very first being. This opinion I have at large examined already; and I suppose what I have said in the foregoing book will be much more easily admitted when I have shown whence the understanding may get all the ideas it has, and by what ways and degrees they may come into the mind, for which I shall appeal to everyone's own observation and experience.

2. Let us then suppose the mind to be, as we say, white paper, void of all characters, without any ideas. How comes it to be furnished? Whence comes it by that vast store which the busy and boundless fancy of man has painted on it with an almost endless variety? Whence has it all the materials of reason and knowledge? To this I answer, in one word, from experience. In that all our knowledge is founded; and from that it ultimately derives itself. Our observation, employed either about external sensible objects or about the internal operations of our minds perceived and reflected on by ourselves, is that which supplies our understandings with all the materials of thinking. These two are the fountains of knowledge, from whence all the ideas we have, or can naturally have, do spring.

3. First, our senses, conversant about particular sensible objects, do convey into the mind several distinct perceptions of things, according to those various ways wherein those objects do affect them. And thus we come by those ideas we have of yellow, white, heat, cold, soft, hard, bitter, sweet, and all those which we call sensible qualities—which, when I say the senses convey into the mind, I mean they from external objects convey into the mind what produces there those perceptions. This great source of most of the ideas we have, depending wholly upon our senses and derived by them to the understanding, I call Sensation.

4. Secondly, the other fountain from which experience furnisheth the understanding with ideas is the perception of the operations of our own mind within us as it is employed about the ideas it has got; which operations, when the soul comes to reflect on and consider, do furnish the understanding with another set of ideas which could not be had from things without. And such are perception, thinking, doubting, believing, reasoning, knowing, willing, and all the different actings of our own minds which we, being conscious of and observing in ourselves, do from these receive into our understandings as distinct ideas as we do from bodies affecting our senses. This source of ideas every man has wholly in himself, and though it be not sense, as having nothing to do with external objects, yet it is very like it and might properly enough be called internal sense. But as I call the other Sensation, so I call this Reflection, the ideas it affords being such only as the mind gets by reflecting on its own operations within itself. By Reflection then, in the following part of this discourse, I would be understood to mean that notice which the mind takes of its own operations, and the manner of them, by reason whereof there come to be ideas of these operations in the understanding. These two, I say, *viz.*, external material things, as the objects of sensation, and the operations of our own minds within, as the objects of reflection, are to me the only originals from whence all our ideas take their beginnings. . . .

*   *   *

6. He that attentively considers the state of a child at his first coming into the world will have little reason to think him stored with plenty of ideas that are to be the matter of his future knowledge. It is by degrees he comes to be furnished with them; and though the ideas of obvious and familiar qualities imprint themselves before the memory begins to keep a register of time or order, yet 'tis often so late before some unusual qualities come in the way that there are few men that cannot recollect the beginning of their acquaintance with them. And if it were worthwhile, no doubt a child might be so ordered as to have but a very few, even of the ordinary ideas, till he were grown up to a man. . . .

Light and colors are busy and at hand everywhere, when the eye is but open; sounds and some tangible qualities fail not to solicit their proper senses and force an entrance to the mind; but yet I think it will be granted easily that if a child were kept in a place where he never saw any other but black and white till he were a man, he would have no more ideas of scarlet or green than he that from his childhood never tasted an oyster or a pineapple has of those particular relishes.

7. Men then come to be furnished with fewer or more simple ideas from without according as the objects they converse with afford greater or less variety; and from the operations of their minds within, according as they more or less reflect on them. For, though he that contemplates the operations of his mind cannot but have plain and clear ideas of them; yet, unless he turn his thoughts that way and considers them attentively, he will no more have clear and distinct ideas of all the operations of his mind and all that may be observed therein than he will have all the particular ideas of any landscape or of the parts and motions of a clock who will not turn his eyes to it and with attention heed all the parts of it. The picture or clock may be so placed that they may come in his way every day; but yet he will have but a confused idea of all the parts they are made up of, till he applies himself with attention to consider them each in particular.

8. And hence we see the reason why 'tis pretty late before most children get ideas of the operations of their own minds, and some have not any very clear or perfect ideas of the greatest part of them all their lives. Because though they pass there continually, yet like floating visions, they make not deep impressions enough to leave in the mind clear, distinct, lasting ideas till the understanding turns inwards upon itself, reflects on its own operations, and makes them the objects of its own contemplation. Children, when they come first into it, are surrounded with a world of new things; which, by a constant solicitation of their senses, draw the mind constantly to them, forward to take notice of new and apt to be delighted with the variety of changing objects. Thus the first years are usually employed and diverted in looking abroad, and acquainting themselves with what is to be found without; and so growing up in a constant attention to outward sensations, [they] seldom make any considerable reflection on what passes within them till they come to be of riper years; and some scarce ever at all.

*   *   *

24. . . . the first capacity of human intellect is that the mind is fitted to receive the impressions made on it, either through the senses by outward objects or by its own operations when it reflects on them. This is the first step a man makes towards the discovery of anything and the groundwork whereon to build all those notions which ever he shall have naturally in this world. All those sublime

thoughts which tower above the clouds and reach as high as heaven itself take their rise and footing here; in all that great extent wherein the mind wanders in those remote speculations it may seem to be elevated with, it stirs not one jot beyond those ideas which sense or reflection have offered for its contemplation.

Part V

LAW, HISTORY, AND POLITICS

An English Disease

In his *Age of Louis XIV* Voltaire remarks that the seventeenth century could well be called "the age of the English." He has in mind the achievements of English science, and especially of Newton; but science was then, as now, international, and it would have been more appropriate to single out the English for special commendation in a field which they sometimes like to pretend is alien to the national genius: political theory. Here especially the English made theoretical discoveries of profound practical consequence.

The reason for this is not far to seek. The English theorists were blessed by a great series of political upheavals and disasters—always the best seedbed for political thought. Florence, in the early sixteenth century, and France later, had produced the most original theorists, stimulated by the death throes of the Florentine republic and by the miseries of the religious wars. Now it was the turn of England—the traditional homeland of political turbulence and instability—to pass through profound constitutional crises which included the decapitation of one king and the deposition of another.

Healthy political organisms generate a minimum of political philosophy. Consider the concept of sovereignty. If it became a serious political question whether Congress could dissolve the President's cabinet by refusing to appropriate any money for the operations of the executive, or what would happen if the President should systematically refuse to enforce the verdicts of the courts, we should rightly suspect that the government was near dissolution. Perhaps we can congratulate ourselves that so few of us would have the first

79

idea as to how to answer such questions. But in England in the early 1640's similar things were happening. The House of Commons refused to supply any money for a war in which Scottish troops had actually invaded the country, then raised their own army because they could not trust the king at the head of the militia. Faced with this collapse of government, even the most hardheaded pragmatists were forced into political theory. As Dr. Johnson says, when a man knows he is to be hanged next morning, it concentrates his mind wonderfully. With a similarly heightened attention, Englishmen turned to those fundamental questions of political obligation and organization which never arise in more tranquil times.

In the seventeenth century, as at most times in human history, authority was easy to take for granted. It was resistance to authority which required rational—and even more, emotional—justification. Political authority was firmly knit into the whole cosmology, so that Copernicus found it natural, at the climax of his *Revolution of the Celestial Orbs,* to speak of the sun "ruling the planets" and to compare it with the election of a Holy Roman Emperor. Indeed, the belief that authority was divinely sanctioned was so much a presupposition of thought that perhaps one sees it better in the unconscious turn of a phrase than in the argumentation of Bossuet or James I (pages 81 and 82). We will understand the political thought of the times better as we become more sensitive to the authoritarian assumptions which underlie even the most fervent appeals for freedom.

These unconscious assumptions should be traced back to the great factory of unconscious ideas, the family, for the basis of all authority lay in the father's power over his family. The essence of the "divine right" theory was that monarchy was hereditary and that the king was entrusted by God with paternal power over his people. This was the basis of the political theory of the royalist Sir Robert Filmer (page 83), but on this point Filmer could draw support even from the suspected Socinian Hugo Grotius (page 83). No matter how radical the thought or action of almost all seventeenth-century revolutionaries, they leave the structure of authority in the family intact. Hobbes merely brushes the question aside; for him, as for the Levellers, the "individual" who is capable of free political action is the head of a family and thus of a smaller political unit over which his authority is virtually absolute. In this respect the truly radical actions of the century were those of the extreme English sectaries who seemed to countenance sexual relationships without marriage, and the truly radical words were those of Milton on divorce (page

84), which call for a divorce law more liberal than those obtaining in most of Europe and America today.

From the stronghold of the family the justification of authority moved outwards to embrace the centers of social and political power. It was easy to quote the Bible: the magistrate did not bear the sword in vain. The majesty of kings was greatly enhanced by the pomp of traditions almost a thousand years old. Even the new cosmology of Kepler and Galileo was more friendly to absolutism than the old hierarchical one. It has been argued that the conception of simple natural laws governing all the matter in the universe was borrowed from that of absolute political sovereignty. Be that as it may, we can be sure that only in a heliocentric cosmology would the suburst have become the emblem of the *Roi soleil,* Louis XIV.

The Scriptures Teach Absolute Monarchy

From Jacques-Bénigne Bossuet, *Principles of Politics Drawn from the Very Words of Holy Scripture* (Paris, 1709), Part I, book iv. Translated from French.

Royal authority is absolute.
To make this term odious and intolerable, some affect to consider absolute government the same as arbitrary government. But there is nothing more dissimilar, as we shall see when we come to speak of justice.

The Prince is not responsible to anyone for what he decrees.
Without this absolute authority, he could neither do good nor put down evil. He must have such power that no one can hope to escape from him; and, finally, the only defense of a private person against the public authority ought to be his innocence.

There is no other judgment above that of princes.
Sovereign judgments are attributed to God Himself. When Jehoshaphat set up judges to judge the people, he said: "You judge not in the name of men, but of God." [2 Chronicles xix, 6] And in Ecclesiastes [viii, 17] we find, "Do not give judgment against the judge." All the more reason not to do so when the judge is the king. . . . We must thus obey princes like justice itself; without this there will be neither justice nor a proper end in human affairs. They are

Gods, and share in some manner the divine independence. "I have said you are Gods, and you are all children of the Most High." [Psalm lxxxii, 6]

Kings as Earthly Gods

From a speech by James I to Parliament, in *Works (London, 1616)*, pp. 529-531.

The state of monarchy is the supremest thing upon earth. For kings are not only God's lieutenants upon earth and sit upon God's throne, but even by God himself they are called gods. There be three principal similitudes that illustrate the state of monarchy: one taken out of the Word of God, and the two other out of the grounds of policy and philosophy. In the Scriptures kings are called Gods, and so their power after a certain relation compared to the divine power. Kings are also compared to fathers of families: for a king is truly *Parens Patriae,* the political father of his people. And lastly kings are compared to the head of this microcosm of the body of man.

Kings are justly called gods for that they exercise a manner or resemblance of divine power upon earth: for if you will consider the attributes of God, you shall see how they agree in the person of a king. God hath power to create or destroy, make or unmake, at his pleasure, and to God are both soul and body due. And the like power have kings: they make and unmake their subjects; they have power to exalt low things and abase high things, and make of their subjects like men at . . . chess—a pawn to take a bishop or a knight, and to cry up or down any of their subjects, as they do their money. . . .

In the first original of kings, whereof some had their beginning by conquest and some by election of the people, their [kings'] wills at that time served for law. Yet how soon kingdoms began to be settled in civility and policy, then did kings set down their minds by laws, which are properly made by the king only, but at the rogation* of the people, the king's grant being obtained thereto. . . . Every just king in a settled kingdom is bound to observe that paction** made to his people by his laws in framing his government

* Formal request
** Bargain or compact

agreeable thereunto. . . . And therefore a king governing in a settled kingdom leaves to be a king and degenerates into a tyrant as soon as he leaves off to rule according to his laws. In which case the king's conscience may speak unto him. . . . And though no Christian man ought to allow any rebellion of people against their Prince, yet doth God never leave kings unpunished when they transgress these limits.

Parents as Earthly Gods

From Grotius, *Rights of War and Peace* (Paris, 1625). Translated from Latin.

. . . Even the very Sacred History (setting aside what consists in precepts) doth not a little provoke us to mutual love, by teaching us that we are all born of the same first parents. . . . Therefore our parents are as gods . . . earthly gods, as Hieracles calls them, conspicuous and visible gods, who do imitate the invisible and unbegotten God, in giving life unto others . . . to whom we owe our reverence as to the gods themselves, saith Aristotle, yet not such an obedience as is infinite and unlimited.

Political Authority Derives from Parental

From Sir Robert Filmer, *Observations upon Aristotle's Politics Touching Forms of Government,* preface.

The first government in the world was monarchical, in the father of all flesh. Adam being commanded to multiply, and people the earth, and to subdue it, and having dominion given him over all creatures, was thereby the monarch of the whole world. None of his posterity had any right to possess anything but by his grant or permission, or by succession from him. "The earth," saith the Psalmist, "hath he given to the children of men": which shows the title comes from fatherhood.

There never was any such thing as an independent multitude who at first had a natural right to a community; this is but a fiction or fancy of too many in these days, who please themselves in running after the opinions of philosophers and poets, to find out such an original of government as might promise them some title of liberty —to the great scandal of Christianity, and bringing in of atheism, since a natural freedom of mankind cannot be supposed without the denial of the creation of Adam. And yet this conceit of original freedom is the only ground upon which not only the heathen philosophers, but also the authors of the principles of the civil law, and Grotius, Selden, Hobbes, Ascham, and others raise and build their doctrines of government and of the several sorts or kinds (as they call them) of commonwealths.

Adam was the Father, King, and Lord over his family; a son, a subject, and a servant or a slave were one and the same thing, at first. . . . I cannot find any one place or text in the Bible where any power or commission is given to a people, either to govern themselves, or to choose themselves governors, or to alter the manner of government at their pleasure. The power of government is settled and fixed by the commandment of "Honor thy Father"; if there were a higher power than the fatherly, then this commandment could not stand and be observed. . . .

Domestic and Political Liberty

From the Preface to John Milton, *The Doctrine and Discipline of Divorce*, 2nd ed. (London, 1644), pp. 2, 4, 6.

He who marries intends as little to conspire his own ruin as he that swears allegiance; and as a whole people is in proportion to an ill government, so is one man to an ill marriage. If they, against any authority, covenant, or statute, may by the sovereign edict of charity save not only their lives but honest liberties from unworthy bondage, as well may he against any private covenant, which he never entered to his mischief, redeem himself upon unsupportable disturbances to honest peace and just contentment. . . . For no effect of tyranny can sit more heavy on the commonwealth than this household unhappiness on the family. And farewell all hope of true reformation in the state while such an evil as this lies undiscerned or unregarded in the house, on the redress whereof depends not only the spiritful and orderly life of our grown men, but the willing and careful education of our children. . . .

What thing [was] more instituted to the solace and delight of man than marriage? And yet the misinterpreting of some scripture directed mainly against the abusers of the law for divorce given by Moses has changed the blessing of matrimony not seldom into a familiar and coinhabiting mischief: at least into a drooping and disconsolate household captivity, without refuge or redemption. . . . Now, if any two be but once handed in the church and have tasted in any sort the nuptial bed, let them find themselves never so mistaken in their dispositions through any error, concealment, or misadventure that through their different tempers, thoughts, and constitutions they can neither be to one another a remedy against loneliness nor live in any union or contentment all their days—yet they shall, so they be but found suitably weaponed to the least possibility of sensual enjoyment,* be made spite of antipathy to fadge together** and combine as they may to their unspeakable wearisomeness and despair of all sociable delight in the ordinance which God established to that very end. . . .

This therefore shall be the task and period of this discourse: to prove, first, that other reasons of divorce besides adultery were by the law of Moses, and are yet to be allowed by the Christian magistrate as a piece of justice, and that the words of Christ were not hereby contraried. Next, that to prohibit absolutely any divorce whatsoever except those which Moses excepted is against the reason of law. . . . This position shall be laid down, first proving, then answering what may be objected either from scripture or light of reason: "That indisposition, unfitness, or contrareity of mind arising from a cause in nature unchangeable, hindering and ever likely to hinder the main benefits of conjugal society, which are solace and peace, is a greater reason of divorce than natural frigidity, especially if there be no children and that there be mutual consent."

The Uses of Erudition

So well entrenched were the arguments for absolute authority that it is an important problem to see how men found the

* Impotence was the most common ground for annulment of marriage in canon law.
** Put up with each other

ideas to counter them.* One source was in the learning—legal, ecclesiastical, and biblical—which was so amply cultivated during the seventeenth century. It is fatally easy for us to drop "the Scientific Revolution" into that slot just after "the Renaissance" and thus forget the continuity between the intellectual preoccupations of the fifteenth and the seventeenth centuries. Erasmus himself had scarcely more passion for Greek than Racine, and there are no finer fruits of the classical legacy than the latter's great tragedies. Milton was a fine enough classical scholar to make an emendation which still stands in a text of Euripides. Hobbes produced a great translation of Thucydides and—in his eighties—one of Homer. In Richard Bentley the English produced the last great classicist to be equally at home in Greek and Latin, and during the seventeenth century gentile scholars made great progress in Hebrew and other Near Eastern languages.

Along with the still lively interest in languages went a more refined skill at textual criticism. Isaac Casaubon deprived the Hermetic writings of the prestige which they had acquired by their imagined association with Moses by showing that they were of a far later date. Richard Simon produced a "critical history"—the word was still something of a novelty—of both the Old and the New Testaments; perhaps the greatest name of all is that of the Benedictine monk Jean Mabillon, whose De Re Diplomatica (1681) proposed methods for authenticating charters so sophisticated that it is possible for the first time to speak of a science of historical scholarship.

We have no reason to think that Mabillon had a greater mind than Lorenzo Valla or Simon than Erasmus. What we have rather is an instance of cumulative knowledge. Scholarship was becoming better organized and more professional, yet without losing its power to fascinate the amateur. Let us recall that Newton spent a good deal more time trying to devise a universal chronology for the history of all people than he devoted to tidying up physics.

This growth of scholarship doubtless owes a good deal to mere curiosity, but scholarship had an important social function and was put to direct political use. For example, the Dutch stood to gain most from the development of a true system of international law, both because the legal status of their revolutionary and republican government was still doubtful and because they were far more dependent on foreign trade for their prosperity than was any other country. It is thus not surprising that Hugh de Groot, more familiar

* Michael Walzer in *The Revolution of the Saints* (1965) makes a stimulating if not altogether convincing case that Puritanism (which this book has had to neglect) was an important source of anti-authoritarian ideas.

to us by his Latin name of Grotius, found uses for his enormous erudition in ransacking virtually the whole of classical literature for examples to establish principles of international jurisprudence.

Like the international law which was just coming into being, the ancient common law of England was uncodified, which meant that success at law required mastering a large number of obscure and ill-digested medieval precedents. Here historical scholarship was scarcely distinguishable from law, and naturally both were far from free of politics.* The confrontation between James I and his Lord Chief Justice, Sir Edward Coke (p. 88) makes the issues plain, but it may not be apparent how revolutionary Coke's position really was. He was discounting the claims of reason in favor of the jurisprudence of an exceedingly complicated "course of the courts" which only a highly skilled attorney could manage: this was professional self-interest. But in denying that the king himself was the highest judge, and indeed the fountain from which all justice flowed, Coke was attacking the oldest tradition in English political life.

The lawyers were claiming that no matter what the will of the king, the common law of England, as interpreted by them, must be the will of the crown. The king could have no personality but his legal one—the state of abnegation achieved by modern British sovereigns. To support this claim they rummaged through the medieval public records, the most complete in Europe, in search of documents showing that the power of kings had always been limited by the common law and parliament. Fortunately it was a case which was not much embarrassed by absence of documents. The oldest and most obscure were interpreted in the light of later ones, and when there were no documents at all, there was no proof that the "ancient constitution" was *not* in force. According to the lawyers, the fundamental aspects of the constitution, as they saw it, were literally of immemorial antiquity. Coke writes learnedly of the parliaments of King Alfred, and he doubtless believed that they met under Alfred's famous but legendary predecessors King Lear and King Cole.

During the first part of the century Coke's vast learning in the laws of England seemed to sweep all before him. The best that Charles I could do was to impound his papers after his death, "being informed there be many extravagant opinions set down there for good law." But in fact Coke's approach to the past was credulous rather than imaginative, and he lacked critical ability. He was as often guilty of wrenching the past to suit his own immediate pur-

---

* See the excellent study by J. G. A. Pocock, *The Ancient Constitution and the Feudal Law* (1957), on which much of this section rests.

poses as was the Long Parliament, which kept a tame antiquarian to dredge up some ancient and undoubted precedent for every step they took in rebellion and regicide.

Meanwhile other scholars, notably the great Sir Henry Spelman, were conducting a more searching investigation of English history. The early maturity of English law and its comparative freedom from Roman influence had meant that there was no reason for English lawyers to know anything of continental law or institutions. But this provincialism was a barrier to proper understanding of English legal history. Men like Spelman who knew something of the legal development of France and Germany could see there institutions akin to those of England. They soon realized that parliament had begun at some specific time in the comparatively recent past. It was seen to be the development of one of the incidents of feudal tenures; and English feudal tenures themselves, they observed, conformed so closely to those found in France that they must have been introduced into England by the Normans at or soon after the Conquest.

This interpretation of English history was obviously a great deal more "royalist" than that of the common lawyers—as well as being a great deal nearer the truth. After the publication of Spelman's manuscripts it came to have more and more acceptance. Thus by the end of the century, though historical precedents were still flung about as the staples of political argument, the defenders of the Stuarts were now capable of giving as good as they got. In fact, the better scholars now adhered to the opinions popularized by Filmer (page 91). The stage was set for John Locke.

Coke on the "Artificial Reason" of the Law

From Sir Edward Coke, *Twelfth Report* (London, 1656), pp. 63-65.

Upon Sunday the tenth of November [1607] . . . the King, upon complaint made to him by Bancroft, Archbishop of Canterbury, concerning prohibitions* . . . was informed that when question was made of what matters the ecclesiastical judges have cognizance . . . the King himself may decide it in his royal person;

* A writ by which a common-law court assumed jurisdiction in a case from an ecclesiastical court.

and that the Judges are but the delegates of the King. . . . And the
Archbishop said that this was clear in Divinity, that such authority
belongs to the King by the Word of God in the Scripture; to which
it was answered by me, in the presence and with the clear consent of
all the Justices of England and Barons of the Exchequer, that the
King in his own person cannot adjudge any case, either criminal, as
treason, felony, etc., or betwixt party and party concerning his inheritance, chattels, or goods, etc., but this ought to be determined
and adjudged in some court of justice according to the law and custom of England.

                    *   *   *

Then the King said that he thought the law was founded upon
reason and that he and others had reason as well as the Judges. To
which it was answered by me, that true it was that God had endowed his Majesty with excellent science and great endowments of
nature, but his Majesty was not learned in the laws of his realm of
England; and causes which concern the life or inheritance or goods
or fortunes of his subjects . . . are not to be decided by natural reason but by the artificial reason and judgment of law, which law is
an art which requires long study and experience before that a man
can attain to the cognizance of it; and that the law was the golden
metewand * and measure to try the causes of the subjects, and which
protected his Majesty in safety and peace. With which the King was
greatly offended and said that then he should be under the law,
which was treason to affirm, as he said; to which I said that Bracton
saith, *quod Rex non debet esse sub homine sed sub Deo et lege.* **

Magna Carta Prohibits Monopolies

From Coke, *Second Part of the Institutes of the Laws of England*
(London, 1642), pp. 45-47.

CAP. XXIX: *No free man shall be taken or imprisoned
or deprived of his freehold, liberties, or free customs; or outlawed
or exiled or in any way destroyed. Nor shall we go or send against*

* Measuring rod
** That the King ought not to be under man, but under God and the law.
Bracton (d. 1268) was an English jurist who wrote the first great commentary on
the common law.

him except by lawful judgment of his peers or by the law of the land. To none shall we sell, deny, or delay justice or right.*

*   *   *

Upon this chapter as out of a root many fruitful branches of the law of England have sprung.

*   *   *

de libertatibus: This word *libertates,* liberties, hath three significations:

1. First, as it hath been said, it signifies the laws of the realm, in which respect this Charter is called *charta libertatum.*

2. It signifies the freedoms that the subjects of England have. For example, the Company of Merchant Tailors of England, having power by their charter to make ordinances, made an ordinance that every brother of the same Society should put the one half of his cloths to be dressed ** by some cloth-maker free of the same company*** . . . and it was adjudged that this ordinance was against law, because it was against liberty of the subject; for every subject hath freedom to put his cloths to be dressed by whom he will.

*   *   *

Generally all monopolies are against this great Charter, because they are against the liberty and freedom of the subject and against the law of the land.

Powers of the House of Commons Limited by Their Writ

From Sir Robert Filmer, *The Free-holder's Grand Inquest* (London, 1679), pp. 5-7.

By this writ we do not find that the Commons are called to be any part of the common council of the kingdom, or of the supreme court of judicature, or to have any part of the legislative power, or to consult *de arduis regni negotiis,* of the difficult business

---

* In Latin in the original.
** Dressing cloth is finishing it so as to give the surface a nap or gloss.
*** Enjoying the full privileges of the company.

of the kingdom. The writ only says, the king would have conference and treat with the prelates, great men, and peers: but not a word of treating or conference with the Commons. . . . Sir Edward Coke, to prove the clergy have no voice in Parliament, says that by the words of their writ their consent was only to such things as were ordained by the common council of the realm. If this argument of his be good, it will deny also voices to the Commons in Parliament, for in their writ are the self-same words, viz. to consent to such things as were ordained by the common council of the kingdom. . . .

For clearing the meaning and sense of the writ, and satisfaction of such as think it impossible but that the Commons of England have always been a part of the common council of the kingdom, I shall insist upon these points: 1. That anciently the barons of England were the common council of the kingdom. 2. That until the time of Henry I [1100-1135] the Commons were not called to Parliament. 3. Though the Commons were called by Henry I yet they were not constantly called, nor yet regularly elected by writ until Henry III's time [1216-1272].

Part VI

HOBBES AND THE
SCIENCE OF POLITICS

Introduction

It would seem that Hobbes, of all people, can speak for himself. He was very conscious of the importance of meaningful and unambiguous discourse, and he wrote some of the most memorable sentences in English prose. Yet the fact that Hobbes is generally remembered as the political philosopher who provided an intellectual justification for the absolute monarchies of his time demonstrates that he has been misunderstood and that his work is neither so clear nor so consistent as it seems.

The brilliance of the pages that Hobbes devotes to political philosophy has helped to obscure the rest of his writings, on which rests his claim to be a systematic philosopher. He tries to reverse the emphasis, describing the *Leviathan* as an interruption of his "speculation of bodies natural," which he expects to be more popular, since "such truth as opposes no man's profit nor pleasure is to all men welcome." In fact, "speculation" was an apt word for his efforts as a natural scientist; despite his claim to have squared the circle, he is alone in the opinion that he was as great a geometer as Descartes. But Hobbes' lack of success as a scientist or a geometer is unimportant; what matters is the coloration which science and geometry gave to his philosophy. It was the discovery of Euclid's forty-seventh theorem which fired his mind with the possibility of moral and political science, and we can see the influence of Galileo's "resolutive-compositive" method in the formulation of his system of politics.

"The skill of making and maintaining commonwealths," he writes, "consists in certain rules, as doth arithmetic and geometry; not, as tennis-play, in practice only." These rules, as he states in the Introduction (p. 95), can be found only in an analysis of the nature of man, the artificer of government and society, and this analysis in turn rests entirely on the examination which every man can make of his own passions. Psychology rather than history must be the basis of political science. Though he was interested in history, Hobbes does not consider it knowledge. Like Descartes, he has no great use for memory, which he defines as "decaying sense." Experience is only a heaping up of memories, and the most that can come of it is prudence. Hobbes does speak of history, and even of what we might call the lessons of history, but only to show that it lacks the certainty required for a foundation of politics:

> . . . he that has seen by what courses and degrees a flourishing state has first come into civil war and then to ruin upon the sight of the ruins of any other state will guess the like war and the like courses have been there also. But this conjecture has the same uncertainty almost with the conjecture of the future, both being grounded only upon experience.

This shows how much difference there is between Hobbes and the Machiavelli of the *Discourses*. If we wish to understand Hobbes, we shall have to remember this total rejection of history. For example, in his discussion of the "state of nature" Hobbes cites the reports of travelers to America who, thanks to the brevity of their visits and their lack of Indian languages, often reported that the Indians had neither government nor property. It may be that he believed there had at one time been a general state of nature such as he describes. But this is irrelevant to his argument and may be confusing; the "state of nature" is one of the "inferences made from the passions," and Hobbes almost always argues it in terms of the *present* relationship between men and between sovereigns. It is derived from "resolution" or analysis of what contemporary civilized life would be like if there were no sovereign authority, and so the force of Hobbes' argument is not diminished even if we find his picture implausible as an anthropological report on primitive man or society.

From his philosophy of science Hobbes also derives his purely naturalistic and mechanistic picture of man as merely matter in motion. Hobbes deserves credit for anticipating Newton; the necessary contrivance of sovereign authority, or Leviathan, is simply the political consequence of the law of the conservation of motion, since it is the way by which every human organism can longest avoid the hazards of collisions with other organisms and postpone its own final quiescence.

It was Hobbes' great and delicate achievement to take the materials of the new science and weave them into a pattern of argument supporting authoritarian (though not absolute) government. No development can have been more astonishing to the conventional supporters of absolute monarchy. Grotius, in *The Rights of War and Peace*, had traced the origin of right to human nature (a rather vaguely defined instinct of "sociability") and argued that his deduction would hold good even if there were no God—which scandalized orthodox opinion. Hobbes now took up a similar, though more radical position, but adroitly turned materialism and the equality of man to the advantage of a sovereign authority, preferably vested in a monarch. He had reason to be pleased with his cleverness, but the monarchists of the time did not share his pleasure. The arguments of such men as Sir Robert Filmer were safer and more convincing, and indeed made better political sense. At the last great book-burning in England, at High Tory Oxford in the days of James II, *Leviathan* figured prominently in the fuel. Charles II kept Hobbes about him, but for his wit and not his counsel. Though there is no doubt that Hobbes personally preferred monarchy to any kind of parliamentary sovereignty, he is always careful to specify that monarchy is simply more convenient. It did not escape contemporary notice that though he was one of the first of Charles I's supporters to flee, he came back when Cromwell was consolidating hs authority, and his arguments could be as serviceable to the general as to the king.

This ability to keep his private political opinions fairly well in their place raises *Leviathan* far above the heaps of political pamphlets spewed out in the English Revolution. The import of his work is really a rational justification of political obligation to sovereign power; the exaggerations which the troubles of the times led him to introduce, such as the unnecessary contention* that the sovereign is not a party to any covenants, can be detached with no harm to the general line of argument. If *Leviathan* were merely another ingenious argument for absolute hereditary monarchy, its present circulation would probably be limited to places such as Saudi Arabia. But the power of abstraction which Hobbes learned from geometry, though it made his doctrines unpalatable and even unrelated to the men of his times, was a wonderful preservative of their philosophical potency. As a profound examination of political obligation, the very basis of the life of men under any government, *Leviathan* must still be reckoned with today.

* So argues Howard Warrender in *The Political Philosophy of Hobbes: His Theory of Obligation* (1957).

Plan of the Leviathan

From the Introduction to Thomas Hobbes, *Leviathan* (London, 1651).

Nature (the art whereby God hath made and governs the world) is by the art of man, as in many other things, so in this also imitated: that it can make an artificial animal. For seeing life is but a motion of limbs, the beginning whereof is in some principal part within, why may we not say that all automata (engines that move themselves by springs and wheels as doth a watch) have an artificial life? For what is the heart but a spring, and the nerves but so many strings, and the joints but so many wheels giving motion to the whole body such as was intended by the artificer? Art goes yet further, imitating that rational and most excellent work of nature, man. For by art is created that great Leviathan called a Commonwealth or State (in Latin *Civitas*) which is but an artificial man, though of greater stature and strength than the natural, for whose protection and defence it was intended; and in which the sovereignty is an artificial soul, as giving life and motion to the whole body; the magistrates and other officers of judicature and execution, artificial joints; reward and punishment (by which, fastened to the seat of the sovereignty, every joint and member is moved to perform his duty) are the nerves, that do the same in the body natural; the wealth and riches of all the particular members are the strength; *salus populi*, the people's safety, its business; counsellors, by whom all things needful for it to know are suggested unto it, are the memory; equity and laws, an artificial reason and will; concord, health; sedition, sickness; and civil war, death. Lastly, the pacts and covenants by which the parts of this body politic were at first made, set together, and united, resemble that *fiat*, or the *let us make man*, pronounced by God in the creation.

To describe the nature of this artificial man, I will consider:

First, the matter thereof and the artificer; both which is man.

Secondly, how, and by what covenants it is made; what are the rights and just power or authority of a sovereign; and what it is that preserves and dissolves it.

Thirdly, what is a Christian commonwealth.

Lastly, what is the Kingdom of Darkness.

Concerning the first, there is a saying much usurped of late, that wisdom is acquired not by reading of books but of men. . . . But there is another saying not of late understood, by which they might learn truly to read one another, if they would take the pains; that is, *nosce teipsum,* read thyself: which was . . . meant . . . to teach us, that . . . whosoever looks into himself and considers what he does when he does think, opine, reason, hope, fear, etc., and upon what grounds, he shall thereby read and know what are the thoughts and passions of all other men upon the like occasions. I say the similitude of passions, which are the same in all men: desire, fear, hope, etc.; not the similitude of the objects of the passions, which are the things desired, feared, hoped, etc.; for these the constitution individual and particular education do so vary and they are so easy to be kept from our knowledge that the characters of man's heart, blotted and confounded as they are with dissembling, lying, counterfeiting, and erroneous doctrines, are legible only to him that searches hearts. And though by men's actions we do discover their design sometimes, yet to do it without comparing them with our own and distinguishing all circumstances by which the case may come to be altered is to decipher without a key, and be for the most part deceived by too much trust or by too much diffidence, as he that reads is himself a good or evil man.

But let one man read another by his actions never so perfectly, it serves him only with his acquaintance, which are but few. He that is to govern a whole nation must read in himself not this or that particular man, but mankind; which though it be hard to do, harder than to learn any language or science; yet when I shall have set down my own reading orderly and perspicuously, the pains left another will be only to consider if he also find not the same in himself. For this kind of doctrine admits no other demonstration.

Man's Perpetual and Restless Desire of Power

From *Leviathan,* chap. **xi.**

. . . The felicity of this life consists not on the repose of a mind satisfied. For there is no . . . *summum bonum* (greatest good) as is spoken of in the books of the old moral philosophers. Nor can a man any more live whose desires are at an end than he whose senses and imaginations are at a stand. Felicity is a continual progress of the desire from one object to another, the attaining of the former being still but the way to the latter. The cause whereof is that the object of man's desire is not to enjoy once only, and for one instant of time; but to assure forever the way of his future desire. And therefore the voluntary actions and inclinations of all men tend not only to the procuring, but also to the assuring of a contented life. . . .

So that in the first place I put for a general inclination of all mankind a perpetual and restless desire of power after power that ceases only in death. And the cause of this is not always that a man hopes for a more intensive delight than he has already attained to, or that he cannot be content with a moderate power: but because he cannot assure the power and means to live well which he has present without the acquisition of more. And from hence it is that kings whose power is greatest turn their endeavors to the assuring it at home by laws or abroad by wars; and when that is done, there succeeds a new desire: in some, of fame from new conquest; in others, of ease and sensual pleasure; in others, of admiration, or being flattered for excellence in some art or other ability of the mind.

The State of Nature

From *Leviathan,* chap. xiii.

Nature has made men so equal in the faculties of the body and mind as that though there be found one man sometimes manifestly stronger in body or of quicker mind than another, yet when all is reckoned together the difference between man and man is not so considerable as that one man can thereupon claim to himself any benefit to which another may not pretend as well as he. For as to the strength of body, the weakest has strength enough to kill the strongest, either by secret machination or by confederacy with others that are in the same danger with himself.

And as to the faculties of the mind, setting aside the arts grounded upon words (and especially that skill of proceeding upon general and infallible rules called science, which very few have, and but in few things) . . . I find yet a greater equality amongst men than that of strength. For prudence is but experience, which equal time equally bestows on all men in those things they equally apply themselves unto. That which may perhaps make such equality incredible is but a vain conceit of one's own wisdom, which almost all men think they have in a greater degree than the vulgar (that is, than all men but themselves and a few others whom by fame or for concurring with themselves they approve). For such is the nature of men that howsoever they may acknowledge many others to be more witty or eloquent or more learned, yet they will hardly believe there be many so wise as themselves; for they see their own wit at hand, and other men's at a distance. But this proves rather that men are in that point equal, than unequal. For there is not ordinarily a greater sign of the equal distribution of anything than that every man is contented with his share.

From this equality of ability arises equality of hope in the attaining of our ends. And therefore if any two men desire the same thing which nevertheless they cannot both enjoy, they become enemies; and in the way to their end—which is principally their own conservation, and sometimes their delectation only—endeavor to destroy or subdue one another. And from hence it comes to pass that where an invader has no more to fear than another man's single power, if one plant, sow, build, or possess a convenient seat, others may probably be expected to come prepared with forces united to dispossess and deprive him not only of the fruit of his labor but also of his life or liberty. And the invader again is in the like danger of another.

And from this diffidence of one another there is no way for any man to secure himself so reasonable as anticipation: that is, by force or wiles to master the persons of all men he can . . . till he see no other power great enough to endanger him; and this is no more than his own conservation requires, and is generally allowed. Also because there be some that [take] pleasure in contemplating their own power in the acts of conquest, which they pursue farther than their security requires, if others that otherwise would be glad to be at ease within modest bounds should not by invasion increase their power, they would not be able [very] long . . . by standing only on their defence, to subsist. And by consequence, such augmentation of dominion over men being necessary to a man's conservation, it ought to be allowed him.

Again, men have no pleasure, but on the contrary a great deal of grief, in keeping company where there is no power able to overawe them all. For every man looks that his companion should value him at the same rate he sets upon himself: and upon all signs of contempt or undervaluing naturally endeavors as far as he dares (which amongst them that have no common power to keep them in quiet is far enough to make them destroy each other) to extort a greater value from his contemners, by damage, and from others, by the example.

So that in the nature of man, we find three principal causes of quarrel. First, competition; secondly, diffidence; thirdly, glory.

The first makes men invade for gain; the second, for safety; and the third, for reputation. The first use violence to make themselves masters of other men's persons, wives, children, and cattle; the second, to defend them; the third, for trifles, as a word, a smile, a different opinion, and any other sign of undervalue, either direct in their persons or by reflection in their kindred, their friends, their nation, their profession, or their name.

Hereby it is manifest that during the time men live without a common power to keep them all in awe they are in that condition which is called war; and such a war as is of every man against every man. For war consists not in battle only or the act of fighting, but in a tract of time wherein the will to contend by battle is sufficiently known; and therefore the notion of time is to be considered in the nature of war as it is in the nature of weather. For as the nature of foul weather lies not in a shower or two of rain, but in an inclination thereto of many days together, so the nature of war consists not in actual fighting, but in the known disposition thereto during all the time there is no assurance to the contrary. All other time is Peace.

Whatsoever therefore is consequent to a time of war, where every man is enemy to every man, the same is consequent to the time wherein men live without other security than what their own strength and their own invention shall furnish them withal. In such condition there is no place for industry, because the fruit thereof is uncertain, and consequently no culture of the earth, no navigation nor use of the commodities that may be imported by sea, no commodious building, no instruments of moving and removing such things as require much force, no knowledge of the face of the earth, no account of time, no arts, no letters, no society, and, which is worst of all, continual fear and danger of violent death; and the life of man solitary, poor, nasty, brutish, and short.

It may seem strange to some man that has not well weighed these things that nature should thus dissociate and render men apt to invade and destroy one another; and he may therefore, not trusting to this inference made from the passions, desire perhaps to have the same confirmed by experience. Let him therefor consider . . . when taking a journey, he arms himself and seeks to go well accompanied; when going to sleep, he locks his doors; when even in his house, he locks his chests; and this when he knows there be laws and public officers armed to revenge all injuries shall be done him—what opinion he has of his fellow-subjects when he rides armed; of his fellow citizens when he locks his doors, and of his children and servants when he locks his chests. Does he not there as much accuse mankind by his actions as I do by my words? But neither of us accuse man's nature in it. The desires and other passions of man are in themselves no sin. No more are the actions that proceed from those passions till they know a law that forbids them: which till laws be made they cannot know, nor can any law be made till they have agreed upon the person that shall make it.

It may peradventure be thought there was never such a time nor condition of war as this; and I believe it was never generally so, over all the world: but there are many places where they live so now. For the savage people in many places of America, except the government of small families, the concord whereof depends on natural lust, have no government at all and live at this day in that brutish manner as I said before. However, it may be perceived what manner of life there would be where there were no common power to fear, by the manner of life which men that have formerly lived under a peaceful government use to degenerate into in a civil war.

But though there had never been any time wherein particular men were in a condition of war one against another, yet in all times kings and person of sovereign authority, because of their independency, are in continual jealousies and in the state and posture of gladiators, having their weapons pointing and their eyes fixed on one another—that is, their forts, garrisons, and guns upon the frontiers of their kingdoms, and continual spies upon their neighbors, which is a posture of war. But because they uphold thereby the industry of their subjects, there does not follow from it that misery which accompanies the liberty of particular men.

To this war of every man against every man this also is consequent: that nothing can be unjust. The notions of right and wrong, justice and injustice, have there no place. Where there is no common power there is no law: where no law, no injustice. Force and fraud are in war the two cardinal virtues. Justice and injustice are . . . faculties neither of the body nor mind. If they were, they might be in a man that were alone in the world, as well as his senses and passions. They are qualities that relate to men in society, not in solitude. It is consequent also to the same condition that there be no propriety, no dominion, no *mine* and *thine* distinct; but only that to be every man's that he can get, and for so long as he can keep it. And thus much for the ill condition which man by mere nature is actually placed in—though with a possibility to come out of it, consisting partly in the passions, partly in his reason.

The passions that incline men to peace are fear of death, desire of such things as are necessary to commodious living, and a hope by their industry to obtain them. And reason suggests convenient articles of peace, upon which men may be drawn to agreement. These articles are they which otherwise are called the Laws of Nature: whereof I shall speak more particularly in the two following chapters.

Covenants

From *Leviathan*, chap. xiv.

The Right of Nature, which writers commonly call *jus naturale,* is the liberty each man has to use his own power as he will himself for the preservation of his own nature—that is to say, of his own life; and consequently of doing anything which in his own judgment and reason he shall conceive to be the aptest means thereunto.

By Liberty is understood, according to the proper signification of the word, the absence of external impediments: which impediments may often take away part of a man's power to do what he would but cannot hinder him from using the power left him according as his judgment and reason shall dictate to him.

A Law of Nature, *lex naturalis,* is a precept or general rule, found out by reason, by which a man is forbidden to do that which is destructive of his life or takes away the means of preserving the same, and to omit that by which he thinks it may be best preserved. For though they that speak of this subject use to confound *jus* and *lex,* right and law, yet they ought to be distinguished; because Right consists in liberty to do or to forbear, whereas Law determines and binds to one of them, so that law and right differ as much as obligation and liberty, which in one and the same matter are inconsistent.

And because the condition of man, as has been declared in the precedent chapter, is a condition of war of everyone against everyone, in which case everyone is governed by his own reason, and there is nothing he can make use of that may not be a help unto him in preserving his life against his enemies; it follows that in such a condition every man has a right to everything, even to one another's body. And therefore, as long as this natural right of every man to everything endures, there can be no security to any man, how strong or wise soever he be, of living out the time which nature ordinarily allows men to live. And consequently it is a precept or general rule of reason that every man ought to endeavor peace, as far as he has hope of obtaining it; and when he cannot obtain it, that he may seek and use all helps and advantages of war. The first branch of which rule contains the first and fundamental law of nature, which is to seek peace and follow it. The second, the sum of the right of nature; which is, by all means we can, to defend ourselves.

From this fundamental law of nature by which men are commanded to endeavor peace is derived this second law: that a man be willing, when others are so too, as far-forth as for peace and defence of himself he shall think it necessary, to lay down this right to all things and be contented with so much liberty against other men as he would allow other men against himself. For as long as every man holds this right of doing anything he likes, so long are all men in the condition of war. But if other men will not lay down their right as well as he then there is no reason for anyone to divest himself of his: for that were to expose himself to prey, which no man is bound to, rather than to dispose himself to peace. This is that law of the Gospel: whatsoever you require that others should do to you, that do ye to them. . . .

To lay down a man's right to anything is to divest himself of the liberty of hindering another of the benefit of his own right to the same. For he that renounces or passes away his right gives not to any other man a right which he had not before, because there is nothing to which every man had not right by nature: but only stands out of his way, that he may enjoy his own original right without hindrance from him . . . So that the effect which redounds to one man by another man's defect of right is but so much diminution of impediments to the use of his own right original.

Right is laid aside either by simply renouncing it or by transferring it to another. By simply renouncing, when he cares not to whom the benefit thereof redounds. By transferring, when he intends the benefit thereof to some certain person or persons. And when a man has in either manner abandoned or granted away his right, then he is said to be obliged or bound not to hinder those to whom such right is granted or abandoned from the benefit of it; and that he ought, and it is his Duty, not to make void that voluntary act of his own; and that such hindrance is Injustice, and Injury, as being *sine jure,* the right being before renounced, or transferred. . . .

Whensoever a man transfers his right or renounces it, it is either in consideration of some right reciprocally transferred to himself or for some other good he hopes for thereby. For it is a voluntary act, and of the voluntary acts of every man, the object is some good to himself. And therefore there be some rights which no man can be understood by any words or other signs to have abandoned or transferred. As first: a man cannot lay down the right of resisting them that assault him by force or take away his life, because he cannot be understood to aim thereby at any good to himself. . . .

*   *   *

The mutual transferring of right is that which men call Contract. . . . one of the contractors may deliver the thing contracted for on his part, and leave the other to perform his part at some determinate time after, and in the mean time be trusted; and then the contract on his part is called a Pact, or Covenant . . .

If a covenant be made wherein neither of the parties perform presently, but trust one another, in the condition of mere nature, which is a condition of war of every man against every man, upon any reasonable suspicion it is void; but if there be a common power set over them both, with right and force sufficient to compel performance, it is not void. For he that performs first has no assurance the other will perform after, because the bonds of words are too weak to bridle men's ambition, avarice, anger, and other passions without the fear of some coercive power—which in the condition of mere nature, where all men are equal and judges of the justness of their own fears cannot possibly be supposed. And therefore he which performs first does but betray himself to his enemy, contrary to the right he can never abandon of defending his life and means of living.

But in a civil estate, where there is a power set up to constrain those that would otherwise violate their faith, that fear is no more reasonable; and for that cause he which by the covenant is to perform first is obliged so to do.

The cause of fear which makes such a covenant invalid must be always something arising after the covenant made, as some new fact or other sign of the will not to perform: else it cannot make the covenant void. For that which could not hinder a man from promising ought not to be admitted as a hindrance of performing.

He that transfers any right transfers the means of enjoying it, as far as lies in his power. . . . And they that give to a man the right of government in sovereignty are understood to give him the right of levying money to maintain soldiers and of appointing magistrates for the administration of justice.

*   *   *

A covenant not to defend myself from force by force is always void. For, as I have showed before, no man can transfer or lay down his right to save himself from death, wounds, and imprisonment, the avoiding whereof is the only end of laying down any right; and therefore the promise of not resisting force in no covenant transfers any right, nor is obliging. For though a man may covenant thus: unless I do so or so, kill me; he cannot covenant thus: unless I do so or so, I will not resist you when you come to kill me. For man by nature chooses the lesser evil, which is danger of death in resisting, rather than the greater, which is certain and present death in not resisting. And this is granted to be true by all men, in that they lead criminals to execution and prison with armed men, notwithstanding that such criminals have consented to the law by which they are condemned.

*   *   *

The force of words being, as I have formerly noted, too weak to hold men to the performance of their covenants, there are in man's nature but two imaginable helps to strengthen it. And those are either a fear of the consequence of breaking their word, or a glory, or pride in appearing not to need to break it. This latter is a generosity too rarely found to be presumed on, especially in the pursuers of wealth, command, or sensual pleasure, which are the greatest part of mankind. The passion to be reckoned upon is fear, whereof there be two very general objects: one, the power of spirits invisible; the other, the power of those men they shall therein offend. Of these two, though the former be the greater power, yet the fear of the latter is commonly the greater fear. The fear of the former is, in every man, his own religion, which has place in the nature of man before civil society. The latter has not so—at least not place enough to keep men to their promises—because in the condition of mere nature the inequality of power is not discerned but by the event of battle. So that before the time of civil society, or in the interruption thereof by war, there is nothing can strengthen a covenant of peace agreed on against the temptations of avarice, ambition, lust, or other strong desire, but the fear of that invisible power which they every one worship as God and fear as a revenger of their perfidy. All therefore that can be done between two men not subject to civil power is to put one another to swear by the God he fears. . . .

The Laws of Nature

From *Leviathan,* chap. xv.

From that law of nature by which we are obliged to transfer to another such rights as, being retained, hinder the peace of mankind, there follows a third, which is this, that men perform their covenants made: without which covenants are in vain and but empty words; and, the right of all men to all things remaining, we are still in the condition of war.

And in this law of nature consists the fountain and original of Justice. For where no covenant has preceded, there has no right been transferred and every man has right to every thing; and consequently, no action can be unjust. But when a covenant is made, then to break it is unjust: and the definition of Injustice is no other than the not performance of covenant. And whatsoever is not unjust is just.

But because covenants of mutual trust, where there is a fear of not performance on either part . . . are invalid; though the original of justice be the making of covenants, yet injustice actually there can be none, till the cause of such fear be taken away, which while men are in the natural condition of war cannot be done. Therefore before the names of just and unjust can have place there must be some coercive power to compel men equally to the performance of their covenants, by the terror of some punishment greater than the benefit they expect by the breach of their covenant, and to make good that propriety which by mutual contract men acquire in recompense of the universal right they abandon; and such power there is none before the erection of a commonwealth.

*　　　　　*　　　　　*

There be some that . . . will not have the law of nature to be those rules which conduce to the preservation of man's life on earth, but to the attaining of an eternal felicity after death—to which they think the breach of covenant may conduce, and consequently be just and reasonable. (Such are they that think it a work of merit to kill or depose or rebel against the sovereign power constituted over them by their own consent.) But because there is no natural knowledge of man's estate after death—much less of the reward that is then to be given to breach of faith—but only a belief grounded upon other men's saying that they know it supernaturally, or that they know those that knew them that knew others that knew it supernaturally, breach of faith cannot be called a precept of reason or nature.

*   *   *

As justice depends on antecedent covenant, so does gratitude depend on antecedent grace—that is to say, antecedent free gift—and is the fourth law of nature, which may be conceived in this form, that a man which receives benefit from another of mere grace endeavor that he which gives it have no reasonable cause to repent him of his good will. For no man gives but with intention of good to himself, because gift is voluntary, and of all voluntary acts, the object is to every man his own good; of which if men see they shall be frustrated there will be no beginning of benevolence or trust, nor consequently of mutual help, nor of reconciliation of one man to another; and therefore they are to remain still in the condition of war, which is contrary to the first and fundamental law of nature, which commands men to seek peace. The breach of this law is called ingratitude and has the same relation to grace that injustice has to obligation by covenant.

A fifth law of nature is complaisance: that is to say, that every man strive to accommodate himself to the rest. . . .

A sixth law of nature is this: that upon caution of the future time, a man ought to pardon the offences past of them that, repenting, desire it. . . .

A seventh is that in revenges (that is, retribution of evil for evil) men look not at the greatness of the evil past, but the greatness of the good to follow. . . .

And because all signs of hatred or contempt provoke to fight, insomuch as most men choose rather to hazard their life than not to be revenged, we may in the eighth place for a law of nature set down this precept: that no man by deed, word, countenance, or gesture declare hatred or contempt of another: the breach of which law is commonly called contumely.

The question who is the better man has no place in the condition of mere nature, where, as has been shown before, all men are equal. The inequality that now is has been introduced by the laws civil. I know that Aristotle in the first book of his *Politics,* for a foundation of his doctrine, makes men by nature some more worthy to command (meaning the wiser sort, such as he thought himself to be for his philosophy); others to serve (meaning those that had strong bodies but were not philosophers as he), as if master and servant were not introduced by consent of men, but by difference of wit—which is not only against reason but also against experience. For there are very few so foolish that had not rather govern themselves than be governed by others: nor when the wise in their own conceit contend by force with them who distrust their own wisdom do they always or often, or almost at any time, get the victory. If nature therefore have made men equal, that equality is to be acknowledged; or if nature have made men unequal, yet because men that think themselves equal will not enter into conditions of peace but upon equal terms, such equality must be admitted. And therefore for the ninth law of nature I put this: that every man acknowledge another for his equal by nature. The breach of this precept is pride.

On this law depends another: that at the entrance into conditions of peace, no man require to reserve to himself any right which he is not content should be reserved to every one of the rest.

*   *   *

These are the laws of nature, dictating peace for a means of the conservation of men in multitudes, and which only concern the doctrine of civil society. . . .

And though this may seem too subtle a deduction of the laws of nature to be taken notice of by all men, whereof the most part are too busy in getting food and the rest too negligent to understand, yet to leave all men inexcusable, they have been contracted into one easy sum, intelligible even to the meanest capacity, and that is, "Do not that to another which you would not have done to yourself."

*   *   *

The laws of nature oblige *in foro interno:* that is to say, they bind to a desire they should take place: but *in foro externo*—that is, to the putting them in act—not always. For he that should be modest and tractable and perform all his promises in such time and place where no one else should do so should but make himself a prey to others and procure his own certain ruin, contrary to the ground of all laws of nature, which tend to nature's preservation. And again, he that having sufficient security that others shall observe the same laws towards him observes them not himself seeks not peace, but war, and consequently the destruction of his nature by violence.

*   *   *

The laws of nature are immutable and eternal; for injustice, ingratitude, arrogance, pride, iniquity, acception of persons,* and the

* Preference of one person above another because of bribery or favoritism.

rest can never be made lawful. For it can never be that war shall preserve life and peace destroy it.

The same laws, because they oblige only to a desire, and endeavor —I mean an unfeigned and constant endeavor—are easy to be observed. For in that they require nothing but endeavor, he that endeavors their performance fulfills them, and he that fulfills the law is just.

And the science of them is the true and only moral philosophy: for moral philosophy is nothing else but the science of what is good and evil in the conversation and society of mankind. Good and evil are names that signify our appetites and aversions, which in different tempers, customs, and doctrines of men are different; and divers men differ not only in their judgment on the senses of what is pleasant and unpleasant to the taste, smell, hearing, touch, and sight, but also of what is conformable or disagreeable to reason in the actions of common life. Nay, the same man, in divers times, differs from himself, and one time praises (that is, calls good) what another time he dispraises, and calls evil: from whence arise disputes, controversies, and at last war. . . . And consequently all men agree on this, that peace is good, and therefore also the way or means of peace (which as I have showed before are justice, gratitude, modesty, equity, mercy, and the rest of the laws of nature) are good—that is to say, moral virtues—and their contrary vices, evil.

*   *   *

These dictates of reason men use to call by the name of laws, but improperly; for they are but conclusions or theorems concerning what conduces to the conservation and defense of themselves; whereas law, properly, is the word of him that by right has command over others. But yet if we consider the same theorems as delivered in the word of God, that by right commands all things, then are they properly called laws.

The Generation of Leviathan

From *Leviathan*, chap. xvii.

The final cause, end, or design of men (who naturally love liberty and dominion over others) in the introduction of that restraint upon themselves in which we see them live in commonwealths is the foresight of their own preservation and of a more contented life thereby: that is to say, of getting themselves out from that miserable condition of war, which is necessarily consequent, as has been shown, to the natural passions of men when there is no visible power to keep them in awe and tie them by fear of punishment to the performance of their covenants and observation of those laws of nature set down in the fourteenth and fifteenth chapters.

For the laws of nature—as justice, equity, modesty, mercy, and, in sum, doing to others as we would be done to—of themselves, without the terror of some power to cause them to be observed, are contrary to our natural passions, that carry us to partiality, pride, revenge, and the like. And covenants without the sword are but words, and of no strength to secure a man at all. . . . If there be no power erected, or not great enough for our security, every man will and may lawfully rely on his own strength and art for caution against all other men. And in all places where men have lived by small families, to rob and spoil one another has been a trade, and so far from being reputed against the law of nature that the greater spoils they gained the greater was their honor. . . . And as small families did then, so now do cities and kingdoms, which are but greater families, for their own security enlarge their dominions upon all pretences of danger and fear of invasion or assistance that may be given to invaders; and endeavor as much as they can to subdue or weaken their neighbors by open force and secret arts—for want of other caution, justly—and are remembered for it in after ages with honor.

*   *   *

And be there never so great a multitude, yet if their actions be directed according to their particular judgments and particular appetites, they can expect thereby no defence nor protection, neither against a common enemy, nor against the injuries of one another. For being distracted in opinions concerning the best use and application of their strength, they do not help but hinder one another, and reduce their strength by mutual opposition to nothing, whereby they are easily not only subdued by a very few that agree together, but also when there is no common enemy they make war upon each other for their particular interests. For if we could suppose a great multitude of men to consent in the observation of justice and other laws of nature without a common power to keep them all in awe, we might as well suppose all mankind to do the same; and then there neither would be nor need to be any civil government or commonwealth at all, because there would be peace without subjection. . . .

It is true that certain living creatures, as bees and ants, live sociably one with another, which are therefore by Aristotle numbered amongst political creatures, and yet have no other direction than their particular judgments and appetites, nor speech, whereby one of them can signify to another what he thinks expedient for the common benefit; and therefore some man may perhaps desire to know why mankind cannot do the same. To which I answer:

First, that men are continually in competition for honor and dignity, which these creatures are not; and consequently amongst men there arises on that ground envy and hatred and finally war; but amongst these not so.

Secondly, that amongst these creatures the common good differs not from the private; and being by nature inclined to their private, they procure thereby the common benefit. But man, whose joy consists in comparing himself with other men, can relish nothing but what is eminent.

Thirdly, that these creatures, having not, as man, the use of reason, do not see nor think they see any fault in the administration of their common business; whereas amongst men there are very many that think themselves wiser and abler to govern the public better than the rest; and these strive to reform and innovate, one this way, another that way; and thereby bring it into distraction and civil war.

Fourthly, that these creatures, though they have some use of voice in making known to one another their desires and other affections, yet they want that art of words by which some men can represent to others that which is good in the likeness of evil and evil in the likeness of good. . . .

Fifthly, irrational creatures cannot distinguish between injury and damage; and therefore as long as they be at ease, they are not offended with their fellows; whereas man is then most troublesome when he is most at ease, for then it is that he loves to show his wisdom and control the actions of them that govern the commonwealth.

Lastly, the agreement of these creatures is natural; that of men is by covenant only, which is artificial; and therefore it is no wonder if there be somewhat else required, besides covenant, to make their agreement constant and lasting, which is a common power to keep them in awe and to direct their actions to the common benefit.

The only way to erect such a common power as may be able to defend them from the invasion of foreigners and the injuries of one another, and thereby to secure them in such sort as that by their own industry and by the fruits of the earth they may nourish themselves and live contentedly, is to confer all their power and strength upon one man, or upon one assembly of men that may reduce all their wills by plurality of voices unto one will: which is as much as to say, to appoint one man or assembly of men to bear their persons, and every one to own and acknowledge himself to be author or whatsoever he that so bears their person shall act, or cause to be acted, in those things which concern the common peace and safety; and therein to submit their wills . . . to his will and their judgments to his judgment. This is more than consent or concord; it is a real unity of them all in one and the same person, made by covenant of every man with every man in such manner as if every man should say to every man, I authorize and give up my right of governing myself to this man or to this assembly of men on this condition, that you give up your right to him and authorize all his actions in like manner. This done, the multitude so united in one person is called a Commonwealth, in Latin *Civitas*. This is the generation of that great Leviathan, or rather, to speak more reverently, of that mortal god, to which we owe under the immortal God our peace and defence. For by this authority, given him by every particular man in the commonwealth, he has the use of so much power and strength conferred on him that by terror thereof he is enabled to perform the wills of them all, to peace at home and mutual aid against their enemies abroad. And in him consists the essence of the commonwealth; which, to define it, is one person of whose acts a great multitude, by mutual covenants one with another, have made themselves every one the author, to the end he may use the strength and means of them all, as he shall think expedient for their peace and common defence.

And he that carries this person is called Sovereign and said to have sovereign power; and every one besides, his Subject.

The attaining to this sovereign power is by two ways. One, by natural force; as when a man makes his children to submit themselves and their children to his government, as being able to destroy them if they refuse; or by war subdues his enemies to his will, giving them their lives on that condition. The other is when men agree amongst themselves to submit to some man or assembly of men voluntarily, on confidence to be protected by him against all others. This latter may be called a political commonwealth or commonwealth by institution, and the former a commonwealth by acquisition. And first I shall speak of a commonwealth by institution.

Powers of the Sovereign

From *Leviathan,* chap. xviii.

A commonwealth is said to be instituted when a multitude of men do agree and covenant, every one with every one, that to whatsoever man or assembly of men shall be given by the major part the right to present the person of them all—that is to say, to be their representative—every one, as well he that voted for it as he that voted against it, shall authorize all the actions and judgments of that man or assembly of men in the same manner as if they were his own, to the end to live peaceably amongst themselves and be protected against other men.

From this institution of a commonwealth are derived all the rights and faculties of him or them on whom the sovereign power is conferred by the consent of the people assembled.

First, because they covenant, it is to be understood they are not obliged by former covenant to any thing repugnant hereunto. And consequently they that have already instituted a commonwealth, being thereby bound by covenant to own the actions and judgments of one, cannot lawfully make a new covenant amongst themselves to be obedient to any other in anything whatsoever, without his permission. And therefore, they that are subjects to a monarch cannot without his leave cast off monarchy and return to the confusion of a disunited multitude, nor transfer their person from him that bears it to another man or other assembly of men; for they are bound, every man to every man, to own and be reputed author of all that he that already is their sovereign shall do . . . and they have also every man given the sovereignty to him that bears their person; and therefore if they depose him, they take from him that which is his own, and so again it is injustice. Besides, if he that attempts to depose his sovereign be killed or punished by him for such attempt, he is author of his own punishment, as being by the institution author of all his sovereign shall do; and because it is injustice for a man to do anything for which he may be punished by his own authority, he is also upon that title unjust. And whereas some men have pretended for their disobedience to their sovereign a new covenant, made not with men, but with God, this also is unjust; for there is no covenant with God but by mediation of somebody that

represents God's person, which none does but God's lieutenant, who
has the sovereignty under God. . . .

Secondly, because the right of bearing the person of them all is
given to him they make sovereign by covenant only of one to another and not of him to any of them, there can happen no breach
of covenant on the part of the sovereign; and consequently none of
his subjects, by any pretense of forfeiture, can be freed from his subjection. That he which is made sovereign makes no covenant with
his subjects beforehand is manifest; because either he must make it
with the whole multitude, as one party to the covenant, or he must
make a several covenant with every man. With the whole as one
party it is impossible, because as yet they are not one person; and
if he make so many several covenants as there be men, those covenants after he has the sovereignty are void, because what act soever
can be pretended by any one of them for breach thereof is the act
both of himself and of all the rest, because done in the person and
by the right of every one of them in particular. Besides, if any one
or more of them pretend a breach of the covenant made by the
sovereign at his institution, and others . . . pretend there was no
such breach, there is in this case no judge to decide the controversy;
it returns therefore to the sword again, and every man recovers the
right of protecting himself by his own strength, contrary to the design they had in the institution. . . . The opinion that any monarch receives his power by covenant—that is to say, on condition—
proceeds from want of understanding this easy truth, that covenants
being but words and breath have no force to oblige, contain, constrain, or protect any man but what it has from the public sword:
that is, from the untied hands of that man or assembly of men that
has the sovereignty and whose actions are avouched by them all
and performed by the strength of them all in him united. . . .

Thirdly, because the major part has by consenting voices declared
a sovereign, he that dissented must now consent with the rest, that
is, be contented to avow all the actions he shall do or else justly be
destroyed by the rest. For if he voluntarily entered into the con-
gregation of them that were assembled, he sufficiently declared
thereby his will and therefore tacitly covenanted to stand to what
the major part should ordain; and therefore if he refuse to stand
thereto or make protestation against any of their decrees, he does
contrary to his covenant and therefore unjustly. . . .

Fourthly, because every subject is by this institution author of all
the actions and judgments of the sovereign instituted, it follows that
whatsoever he does, it can be no injury to any of his subjects, nor
ought he to be by any of them accused of injustice. For he that does

anything by authority from another does therein no injury to him by whose authority he acts; but by this institution of a commonwealth every particular man is author of all the sovereign does; and consequently he that complains of injury from his sovereign complains of that whereof he himself is author; and . . . to do injury to one's self is impossible. It is true that they that have sovereign power may commit iniquity, but not injustice or injury in the proper signification.

Fifthly, and consequently to that which was said last, no man that has sovereign power can justly be put to death, or otherwise in any manner by his subjects punished. . . .

Sixthly, it is annexed to the sovereignty to be judge of what opinions and doctrines are averse, and what conducing to peace; and consequently, on what occasions, how far, and what men are to be trusted withal in speaking to multitudes of people; and who shall examine the doctrines of all books before they be published. For the actions of men proceed from their opinions, and in the well-governing of opinions consists the well-governing of men's actions. . . . And though in matter of doctrine nothing ought to be regarded but the truth, yet this is not repugnant to regulating the same by peace. For doctrine repugnant to peace can no more be true than peace and concord can be against the law of nature. It is true that in a commonwealth where by the negligence or unskilfulness of governors and teachers false doctrines are by time generally received, the contrary truths may be generally offensive. Yet the most sudden and rough bustling in of a new truth that can be does never break the peace, but only sometimes awake the war. For those men that are so remissly governed that they dare take up arms to defend or introduce an opinion are still in war, and their condition not peace, but only a cessation of arms for fear of one another; and they live, as it were, in the precincts of battle continually. It belongs therefore to him that has the sovereign power to be judge or constitute all judges of opinions and doctrines, as a thing necessary to peace, thereby to prevent discord and civil war.

Seventhly is annexed to the sovereignty the whole power of prescribing the rules whereby every man may know what goods he may enjoy and what actions he may do without being molested by any of his fellow-subjects; and this is it men call propriety. . . .

Eighthly is annexed to the sovereignty the right of judicature. . . . For without the decision of controversies, there is no protection of one subject against the injuries of another . . .

Ninthly is annexed to the sovereignty the right of making war and peace with other nations and commonwealths. . . .

Tenthly is annexed to the sovereignty the choosing of all counsellors, ministers, magistrates, and officers, both in peace and
war. . . .

Eleventhly, to the sovereign is committed the power of rewarding
with riches or honor and of punishing with corporal or pecuniary
punishment or with ignominy every subject. . . .

Lastly, considering what value men are naturally apt to set upon
themselves, what respect they look for from others, and how little
they value other men, from whence continually arise amongst them
emulation, quarrels, factions, and at last war, to the destroying of
one another and diminution of their strength against a common
enemy, it is necessary that there be laws of honor and a public rate
of the worth of such men as have deserved or are able to deserve
well of the commonwealth. . . .

These are the rights which make the essence of sovereignty and
which are the marks whereby a man may discern in what man or
assembly of men the sovereign power is placed and resides. For these
are incommunicable and inseparable. The power to coin money, to
dispose of the estate and persons of infant heirs, to have pre-emption
in markets, and all other statute prerogatives may be transferred by
the sovereign, and yet the power to protect his subjects be retained.
But if he transfer the militia, he retains the judicature in vain, for
want of execution of the laws; or if he grant away the power of
raising money, the militia is in vain; or if he will give away the government of doctrines, men will be frighted into rebellion with the
fear of spirits. . . . And this division is it whereof it is said, "a
kingdom divided in itself cannot stand": for unless this division
precede, division into opposite armies can never happen. If there
had not first been an opinion received of the greatest part of England that these powers were divided between the king and the Lords
and the House of Commons, the people had never been divided
and fallen into this civil war. . . .

Natural and Political Liberty

From *Leviathan,* chap. xxi.

Liberty or Freedom signifies properly the absence of opposition. By opposition I mean external impediments of motion;
and [this] may be applied no less to irrational and inanimate crea-

tures than to rational. For whatsover is so tied or environed as it cannot move but within a certain space, which space is determined by the opposition of some external body, we say it has not liberty to go further. And so of all living creatures, while they are imprisoned or restrained with walls or chains; and of the water while it is kept in by banks or vessels that otherwise would spread itself into a larger space, we . . . say they are not at liberty to move in such manner as without those external impediments they would. But when the impediment of motion is in the constitution of the thing itself, we [do] not . . . say it wants the liberty, but the power to move; as when a stone lies still or a man is fastened to his bed by sickness. . . .

But when the words *free* and *liberty* are applied to anything but bodies, they are abused; for that which is not subject to motion is not subject to impediment; and therefore when it is said, for example, the way is free, no liberty of the way is signified, but of those that walk in it without stop. . . . Lastly, from the use of the word *free-will* no liberty can be inferred of the will, desire, or inclination, but the liberty of the man, which consists in this: that he finds no stop in doing what he has the will, desire, or inclination to do.

Fear and liberty are consistent, as when a man throws his goods into the sea for fear the ship should sink; he does it nevertheless very willingly, and may refuse to do it if he will. It is therefore the action of one that was free. . . .

Liberty and necessity are consistent, as in the water that has not only liberty, but a necessity of descending by the channel. So likewise in the actions which men voluntarily do, which, because they proceed from their will, proceed from liberty; and yet, because every act of man's will and every desire and inclination proceeds from some cause, and that from another cause, in a continual chain whose first link is in the hand of God the first of all causes, proceed from necessity. So that to him that could see the connection of those causes the necessity of all men's voluntary actions would appear manifest. . . . And this shall suffice, as to the matter in hand, of that natural liberty which only is properly called liberty.

But as men for the attaining of peace and conservation of themselves thereby have made an artificial man, which we call a commonwealth, so also have they made artificial chains, called civil laws. . . .

In relation to these bonds only it is that I am to speak now of the liberty of subjects. For seeing there is no commonwealth in the world wherein there be rules enough set down for the regulating of all the actions and words of men, as being a thing impossible, it follows necessarily that in all kinds of actions by the laws praetermitted* men have the liberty of doing what their own reasons shall suggest. . . . For if we take liberty in the proper sense for corporal liberty—that is to say, freedom from chains and prison—it were very absurd for men to clamor as they do for the liberty they so manifestly enjoy. Again, if we take liberty for an exemption from laws, it is no less absurd for men to demand as they do that liberty by which all other men may be masters of their lives. . . . The liberty of a subject lies therefore only in those things which in regulating their actions the sovereign has praetermitted: such as . . . the liberty to buy and sell and otherwise contract with one another, to choose their own abode, their own diet, their own trade of life, and institute** their children as they themselves think fit, and the like.

Nevertheless we are not to understand that by such liberty the sovereign power of life and death is either abolished or limited. . . . And therefore it may and does often happen in commonwealths that a subject may be put to death by the command of the sovereign power, and yet neither do the other wrong. . . . And the same holds also in a sovereign prince that puts to death an innocent subject. For though the action be against the law of nature, as being contrary to equity, as was the killing of Uriah by David, yet it was not an injury to Uriah, but to God. Not to Uriah, because [David's] right to do what he pleased was given him by Uriah himself; and yet to God, because David was God's subject and prohibited [from] all iniquity by the law of nature—which distinction David himself, when he repented the fact, evidently confirmed, saying, "To Thee only have I sinned."

*   *   *

To come now to the particulars of the true liberty of a subject (that is to say, what are the things which though commanded by the sovereign he may nevertheless without injustice refuse to do) we are to consider what rights we pass away when we make a commonwealth, or—which is all one—what liberty we deny ourselves by owning all the actions without exception of the man or assembly we make our sovereign. . . .

First, therefore, seeing sovereignty by institution is by covenant of everyone to everyone, and sovereignty by acquisition by covenants of the vanquished to the victor or child to the parent, it is manifest that every subject has liberty in all those things the right whereof

* Overlooked
** Educate

cannot by covenant be transferred. I have shown before . . . that covenants not to defend a man's own body are void. Therefore:

If the sovereign command a man, though justly condemned, to kill, wound, or maim himself, or not to resist those that assault him, or to abstain from the use of food, air, medicine, or any other thing without which he cannot live, yet has that man the liberty to disobey.

If a man be interrogated . . . concerning a crime done by himself, he is not bound, without assurance of pardon, to confess it. . . .

Again, the consent of a subject to a sovereign power is contained in these words: I authorize, or take upon me, all his actions; in which there is no restriction at all of his own former natural liberty: for by allowing him to kill me, I am not bound to kill myself when he commands me. . . .

Upon this ground a man that is commanded as a soldier to fight against the enemy, though his sovereign have right enough to punish his refusal with death, may nevertheless in many cases refuse without injustice; as when he substitutes a sufficient soldier in his place; for in this case he deserts not the service of the commonwealth. And there is allowance to be made for natural timorousness, not only to women, of whom no such dangerous duty is expected, but also to men of feminine courage. When armies fight, there is on one side, or both, a running away; yet when they do it not out of treachery, but fear, they are not esteemed to do it unjustly, but dishonorably.

*   *   *

The obligation of subjects to the sovereign is understood to last as long, and no longer, than the power lasts by which he is able to protect them. For the right men have by nature to protect themselves, when none else can protect them, can by no covenant be relinquished. The sovereignty is the soul of the commonwealth, which once departed from the body, the members do no more receive their motion from it. The end of obedience is protection, which, wheresoever a man sees it—either in his own or in another's sword—nature applies his obedience to it and his endeavor to maintain it. And though sovereignty, in the intention of them that make it, be immortal, yet it is in its own nature not only subject to violent death, by foreign war, but also through the ignorance and passions of men it has in it, from the very institution, many seeds of a natural mortality, by intestine discord.

Part VII

THE RIGHTS OF MAN
AND OF MERCHANT

Introduction

Hobbes' *Leviathan* and Locke's *Two Treatises of Government* are generally taken to be the two landmarks of seventeenth-century political thought; but they have lived for opposite reasons. Hobbes' greatness lay in his ability to dissolve the confusions and controversies of his time by an analysis which laid bare the fundamental philosophical issues. As we have seen, the few intrusions of his own political feelings only spoiled the clarity of his arguments, and his lack of any immediate political impact made no difference to his ultimate influence. Locke, on the other hand, often embraced the confusions and plunged into most of the controversies of his time. Had his work met the blank incomprehension that Hobbes encountered, it would have been virtually worthless; but Locke, who perhaps failed to make a great contribution to political philosophy, amply succeeded in the more potent achievement of formulating a political ideology.

Locke's *Two Treatises of Government,* as everyone knows, were tracts for the times—though not everyone knows which times. (Although they were published in 1690 to help vindicate the parliamentary title of William III, they were substantially written from 1679 to 1681 to provide argument for excluding James from the succession to the English throne.)* Since he was striving for maximum

---

* This explains the importance Locke gives to such things as parliamentary reform, which were issues in this Exclusion Crisis but not in the Glorious Revolution. Locke's *Second Treatise* was considerably more radical than William III's cause really required. See the arguments establishing the dating in the preface

political effect, Locke was not above sacrificing truth for persuasion. For example, he speaks of innate ideas "writ in the hearts" of men in the state of nature, though in the same year that the (anonymous) *Second Treatise* appeared another treatise was published by John Locke, gentleman, demonstrating that such innate ideas do not exist. The *Second Treatise* is not even internally consistent, since the word "property" is used ambiguously, and it is hard to know what to make of the apparent existence of wage labor in the state of nature (page 127).

Such fallacies and inconsistencies are the ordinary stuff of political tracts, and they are usually excused in being forgotten. But Locke's work was—deservedly—not forgotten. He knew his audience, and knew that he alone could reach it. He had no legal or historical training and thus was unable to counter the royalist historians and lawyers who were now showing that parliament was itself a creation of the monarchy. He was virtually the only pamphleteer on either side of the Exclusion controversy who does not argue his case mainly in terms of English constitutional law and precedent. But this was in fact an advantage; since the historical argument had gone sour, it was necessary to reformulate the case against royal absolutism in a way which was not confined to the mystique of the legal profession or vulnerable to the advances of historical scholarship. The common law was—in more than one sense of the word—the law of the land, and the common-law arguments were consonant with the mental habits of the English landowners. But Locke, himself a substantial stockholder in various commercial ventures, framed his argument in terms which would appeal to the mercantile community. He said— without bothering to admit that he had written it—that the treatment of property (page 126) was the best thing he had ever read on that subject. Naturally it spoke with particular force to those "rational and industrious" entrepreneurs who asked of government only that it provide a dependable legal structure in which they could reap their fair rewards.*

The tones of utility and rational calculation which Locke sounded were also uniquely suited to be heard outside England. While better acquaintance with continental history had weakened the force of the common-law argument, Locke, by detaching his arguments from history, made them available for application and use anywhere.

---

to Peter Laslett's edition of Locke's *Two Treatises of Government* (Cambridge University Press, 1963). All selections from the *Second Treatise* are taken from this edition.

   * The aspects of this are ingeniously developed in C. B. McPherson, *The Political Theory of Possessive Individualism* (1962).

The *Second Treatise* was to be the vehicle by which the political experience of seventeenth-century England passed into the general European consciousness. It was almost immediately translated into French and passed through six further editions in French before 1789, as well as an Italian, a German, and a Swedish translation. The latter appeared shortly after the Swedish nobility had defeated their monarch and was a tribute to their tastes in self-justifications. But as events in France later in the century were to show, the *Second Treatise* was not merely one of those books which provide convenient rationalizations for what has already been done. It was rather one of those which Milton described: "as lively and as vigorously productive as those fabulous dragon's teeth; and being sown up and down, may chance to spring up armed men."

The Definition of Political Power

From John Locke, *Second Treatise of Government* (London, 1690), chap. i.

It having been shown in the foregoing Discourse:
(1) That Adam had not either by natural Right of Fatherhood or by positive donation from God any such authority over his children or dominion over the world as is pretended.
(2) That if he had, his heirs yet had no right to it.
(3) That if his heirs had, there being no law of Nature nor positive law of God that determines which is the right heir in all cases that may arise, the right of succession and consequently of bearing rule could not have been certainly determined.
(4) That if even that had been determined, yet the knowledge of which is the eldest line of Adam's posterity being so long since utterly lost . . . in the races of mankind and families of the world, there remains not to one above another the least pretense to be the eldest house and to have the right of inheritance.

All these premises having, as I think, been clearly made out, it is impossible that the rulers now on earth should make any benefit or derive any the least shadow of authority from that which is held to be the fountain of all power, Adam's private dominion and paternal jurisdiction; so that he that will not give just occasion to think that all government in the world is the product only of force and violence and that men live together by no other rules but that of beasts . . . must of necessity find out another rise of government, another original of political power, and another way of designing and knowing the persons that have it than what Sir Robert F[ilmer] hath taught us.

2. To this purpose, I think it may not be amiss to set down what I take to be political power, that the power of a magistrate over a subject may be distinguished from that of a father over his children, a master over his servant, a husband over his wife, and a lord over his slave. All which distinct powers happening sometimes together in the same man, if he be considered under these different relations, it may help us to distinguish these powers one from another, and show the difference betwixt a ruler of a commonwealth, a father of a family, and a captain of a galley.

3. Political power then I take to be a right of making laws with penalties of death, and consequently all less penalties, for the regulating and preserving of property and of employing the force of the community in the execution of such laws and in the defence of the commonwealth from foreign injury, and all this only for the public good.

The State of Nature

From the *Second Treatise of Government*, chap. ii.

4. To understand political power right and derive it from its original, we must consider what state all men are naturally in; and that is a state of perfect freedom to order their actions and dispose of their possessions and persons as they think fit, within the bounds of the law of nature, without asking leave or depending upon the will of any other man.

A state also of equality, wherein all the power and jurisdiction is reciprocal, no one having more than another; there being nothing more evident than that creatures of the same species and rank promiscuously born to all the same advantages of nature and the use of the same faculties should also be equal one amongst another without subordination or subjection, unless the lord and master of them all should by any manifest declaration of his will set one above another, and confer on him by an evident and clear appointment an undoubted right to dominion and sovereignty.

5. This equality of men by nature the judicious Hooker* looks upon as so evident in itself and beyond all question that he makes it the foundation of that obligation to mutual love amongst men on which he builds the duties they owe one another, and from whence he derives the great maxims of justice and charity.

6. But though this be a state of liberty, yet it is not a state of license. Though man in that state have an uncontrollable liberty to dispose of his person or possessions, yet he has not liberty to destroy himself, or so much as any creature in his possession, but where some nobler use than its bare preservation calls for it. The state of nature has a law of nature to govern it, which obliges every one: and reason, which is that law, teaches all mankind who will but consult it that being all equal and independent, no one ought to harm another in his life, health, liberty, or possessions. For men being all the workmanship of one omnipotent and infinitely wise maker, all the servants of one sovereign master sent into the world by his order and about his business, they are his property whose workmanship they are—made to last during his, not one another's pleasure. And being furnished with like faculties, sharing all in one community of nature, there cannot be supposed any such subordination among us that may authorize us to destroy one another, as if we were made for one another's uses as the inferior ranks of creatures are for ours. Everyone as he is bound to preserve himself and not to quit his station wilfully, so by the like reason when his own preservation comes not in competition ought he as much as he can to preserve the rest of mankind, and may not, unless it be to do justice on an offender, take away or impair the life or what tends to the preservation of the life, the liberty, health, limb or goods of another.

7. And that all men may be restrained from invading others' rights and from doing hurt to one another, and the law of nature be observed, which willeth the peace and preservation of all mankind, the execution of the law of nature is in that state put into every man's hands, whereby everyone has a right to punish the transgressors of that law to such a degree as may hinder its violation. For the law of nature would, as all other laws that concern men in this world, be in vain if there were nobody that in the state of nature had a power to execute that law and thereby preserve the innocent and restrain offenders; and if anyone in the state of nature may punish another for any evil he has done, everyone may do so. For in that

* Richard Hooker (1553-1600), author of the *Laws of Ecclesiastical Polity*, the classic defense of the Church of England. Locke, otherwise not much given to quotation, often cites Hooker, though it appears he had not even finished the first of the eight books of the *Ecclesiastical Polity*.

state of perfect equality, where naturally there is no superiority or jurisdiction of one over another, what any may do in prosecution of that law everyone must needs have a right to do.

8. And thus in the state of nature one man comes by a power over another; but yet no absolute or arbitrary power to use a criminal when he had got him in his hands according to the passionate heats or boundless extravagancy of his own will, but only to retribute to him, so far as calm reason and conscience dictates, what is proportionate to his transgression, which is so much as may serve for reparation and restraint. For these two are the only reasons why one man may lawfully do harm to another, which is that we call punishment. In transgressing the law of nature, the offender declares himself to live by another rule than that of reason and common equity, which is that measure God has set to the actions of men for their mutual security; and so he becomes dangerous to mankind, the tie which is to secure them from injury and violence being slighted and broken by him. Which being a trespass against the whole species and the peace and safety of it provided for by the law of nature, every man upon this score, by the right he hath to preserve mankind in general, may restrain, or where it is necessary, destroy things noxious to them, and so may bring such evil on anyone who hath transgressed that law as may make him repent the doing of it, and thereby deter him, and by his example others, from doing the like mischief. And in this case, and upon this ground, every man hath a right to punish the offender and be executioner of the law of nature.

9. I doubt not but this will seem a very strange doctrine to some men; but before they condemn it, I desire them to resolve me by what right any prince or state can put to death or punish an alien for any crime he commits in their country. 'Tis certain their laws by virtue of any sanction they receive from the promulgated will of the legislature, reach not a stranger. . . . Those who have the supreme power of making laws in England, France, or Holland are to an Indian but like the rest of the world: men without authority; and therefore if by the law of nature every man hath not a power to punish offense against it, as he soberly judges the case to require, I see not how the magistrates of any community can punish an alien of another country, since in reference to him they can have no more power than what every man naturally may have over another.

*   *   *

13. To this strange doctrine, *viz.,* that in the state of nature everyone has the executive power of the law of nature, I doubt not but it will be objected that it is unreasonable for men to be judges in their

own cases, that self-love will make men partial to themselves and their friends. And on the other side, that ill nature, passion, and revenge will carry them too far in punishing others. And hence nothing but confusion and disorder will follow; and that therefore God hath certainly appointed government to restrain the partiality and violence of men. I easily grant that civil government is the proper remedy for the inconveniences of the state of nature, which must certainly be great where men may be judges in their own case, since 'tis easily to be imagined that he who was so unjust as to do his brother an injury will scarce be so just as to condemn himself for it. But I shall desire those who make this objection to remember that absolute monarchs are but men, and if government is to be the remedy of those evils which necessarily follow from men's being judges in their own cases, and the state of nature is therefore not to be endured, I desire to know what kind of government that is, and how much better it is than the state of nature, where one man commanding a multitude has the liberty to be judge in his own case and may do to all his subjects whatever he pleases, without the least liberty to anyone to question or control those who execute his pleasure? And in whatsoever he doth, whether led by reason, mistake, or passion, must be submitted to? Much better it is in the state of nature wherein men are not bound to submit to the unjust will of another: and if he that judges, judges amiss in his own or any other case, he is answerable for it to the rest of mankind.

14. 'Tis often asked as a mighty objection: Where are, or ever were, there any men in such a state of nature? To which it may suffice as an answer at present that since all princes and rulers of independent governments all throughout the world are in a state of nature, 'tis plain the world never was nor ever will be without numbers of men in that state. I have named all governors of independent communities, whether they are or are not in league with others; for 'tis not every compact that puts an end to the state of nature between men, but only this one of agreeing together mutually to enter into one community and make one body politic; other promises and compacts men may make one with another and yet still be in the state of nature. The promises and bargains for truck, etc., between the two men in the desert island, mentioned by Garcilasso de la Vega in his *History of Peru,* or between a Swiss and an Indian in the woods of America, are binding to them, though they are perfectly in a state of nature in reference to one another. For truth and keeping of faith belongs to men as men, and not as members of society.

15. To those that say there were never any men in the state of nature, I will not only oppose the authority of the judicious Hooker,

Eccl. Pol. Lib. 1 Sect. 10, where he says: ". . . the laws of nature do bind men absolutely, even as they are men, although they have never any settled fellowship, never any solemn agreement amongst themselves what to do or not to do, but for as much as we are not by our selves sufficient to furnish our selves with competent store of things needful for such a life as our nature doth desire, a life fit for the dignity of man; therefore to supply those defects and imperfections which are in us, as living singly and solely by our selves, we are naturally induced to seek communion and fellowship with others. This was the cause of men's uniting themselves at first in politic societies." But I moreover affirm that all men are naturally in that state, and remain so till by their own consents they make themselves members of some politic society; and I doubt not in the sequel of this discourse to make it very clear.

Property

From the *Second Treatise of Government,* chap. **v.**

25. Whether we consider natural reason, which tells us that men being once born have a right to their preservation and consequently to meat and drink and such other things as nature affords for their subsistence, or revelation, which gives us an account of those grants God made of the world to Adam and to Noah and his sons, 'tis very clear that God, as King David says (Psalm 115, 16) "has given the earth to the children of men," given it to mankind in common. But this being supposed, it seems to some a very great difficulty how anyone should ever come to have a property in anything. I will not content myself to answer that if it be difficult to make out property upon a supposition that God gave the world to Adam and his posterity in common, it is impossible that any man but one universal monarch should have any property upon a supposition that God gave the world to Adam and his heirs in succession, exclusive of all the rest of his posterity. But I shall endeavor to show how men might come to have a property in several parts of that which God gave to mankind in common, and that without any express compact of all the commoners.

26. God, who hath given the world to men in common, hath also given them reason to make use of it to the best advantage of life and convenience. The earth and all that is therein is given to men

for the support and comfort of their being. And though all the fruits it naturally produces and beasts it feeds belong to mankind in common, as they are produced by the spontaneous hand of nature, and nobody has originally a private dominion exclusive of the rest of mankind in any of them, as they are thus in their natural state; yet being given for the use of men, there must of necessity be a means to appropriate them some way or other before they can be of any use or at all beneficial to any particular man. . . .

27. Though the earth and all inferior creatures be common to all men, yet every man has a property in his own person. This nobody has any right to but himself. The labor of his body and the work of his hands, we may say, are properly his. Whatsoever then he removes out of the state that nature hath provided and left it in, he hath mixed his labor with and joined to it something that is his own, and thereby makes it his property. . . .

28. He that is nourished by the acorns he picked up under an oak or the apples he gathered from the trees in the wood has certainly appropriated them to himself. Nobody can deny but the nourishment is his. I ask then, when did they begin to be his? when he digested? or when he ate? or when he boiled? or when he brought them home? or when he picked them up? And 'tis plain if the first gathering made them not his, nothing else could. That labor put a distinction between them and common. That added something to them more than nature, the common mother of all, had done; and so they became his private right. And will anyone say he had no right to those acorns or apples he thus appropriated because he had not the consent of all mankind to make them his? Was it a robbery thus to assume to himself what belonged to all in common? If such a consent as that was necessary, man had starved notwithstanding the plenty God had given him. We see in commons which remain so by compact that 'tis the taking any part of what is common and removing it out of the state nature leaves it in which begins the property, without which the common is of no use. And the taking of this or that part does not depend on the express consent of all the commoners. Thus the grass my horse has bit, the turfs my servant has cut, and the ore I have dug in any place where I have a right to them in common with others become my property without the assignation or consent of anybody.

*   *   *

30. Thus the law of reason makes the deer that Indian's who hath killed it; 'tis allowed to be his goods who hath bestowed his labor upon it, though before it was the common right of everyone. And

amongst those who are counted the civilized part of mankind, who have made and multiplied positive laws to determine property, this original law of nature for the beginning of property in what was before common still takes place; and by virtue thereof, what fish anyone catches in the ocean, that great and still remaining common of mankind, or what ambergris anyone takes up here is, by the labor that removes it out of that common state nature left it in, made his property who takes that pains about it. And even amongst us the hare that anyone is hunting is thought his who pursues her during the chase. For being a beast that is still looked upon as common, and no man's private possession, whoever has employed so much labor about any of that kind as to find and pursue her has thereby removed her from the state of nature wherein she was common and hath begun a property.

31. It will perhaps be objected to this that if gathering the acorns or other fruits of the earth, etc., makes a right to them, then anyone may engross as much as he will. To which I answer, not so. The same law of nature that does by this means give us property does also bound that property too. "God has given us all things richly" (1 Tim. vi. 17) is the voice of reason confirmed by inspiration. But how far has he given it us? To enjoy. As much as anyone can make use of to any advantage of life before it spoils, so much he may by his labor fix a property in. Whatever is beyond this is more than his share, and belongs to others. Nothing was made by God for man to spoil or destroy. And thus considering the plenty of natural provisions there was a long time in the world, and the few spenders, and to how small a part of that provision the industry of one man could extend itself and engross it to the prejudice of others—especially keeping within the bounds set by reason of what might serve for his use—there could be then little room for quarrels or contentions about property so established.

32. But the chief matter of property being now not the fruits of the earth and the beasts that subsist on it, but the earth itself, as that which takes in and carries with it all the rest, I think it is plain that property in that too is acquired as the former. As much land as a man tills, plants, improves, cultivates, and can use the product of, so much is his property. He by his labor does, as it were, enclose it from the common. . . .

33. Nor was this appropriation of any parcel of land by improving it any prejudice to any other man, since there was still enough and as good left, and more than the yet unprovided could use. So that in effect there was never the less left for others because of his en-

closure for himself. For he that leaves as much as another can make use of does as good as take nothing at all. Nobody could think himself injured by the drinking of another man, though he took a good draught, who had a whole river of the same water left him to quench his thirst. And the case of land and water, where there is enough of both, is perfectly the same.

34. God gave the world to men in common; but since he gave it them for their benefit and the greatest conveniences of life they were capable to draw from it, it cannot be supposed he meant it should always remain common and uncultivated. He gave it to the use of the industrious and rational (and labor was to be his title to it); not to the fancy or covetousness of the quarrelsome and contentious. He that had as good left for his improvement as was already taken up needed not complain [and] ought not to meddle with what was already improved by another's labor. If he did, 'tis plain he desired the benefit of another's pains, which he had no right to, and not the ground which God had given him in common with others. . . .

36. The measure of property nature has well set by the extent of men's labor and the conveniency of life. No man's labor could subdue or appropriate all, nor could his enjoyment consume more than a small part, so that it was impossible for any man this way to entrench upon the right of another or acquire to himself a property to the prejudice of his neighbor, who would still have room for as good and as large a possession (after the other had taken out his) as before it was appropriate[d]. This measure did confine every man's possession to a very moderate proportion and such as he might appropriate to himself without injury to anybody in the first ages of the world, when men were more in danger to be lost by wandering from their company in the then vast wilderness of the earth than to be straitened for want of room to plant in. And the same measure may be allowed still without prejudice to anybody, as full as the world seems. For supposing a man or family in the state they were at first peopling of the world by the children of Adam or Noah, let him plant in some inland vacant places of America: we shall find that the possessions he could make himself upon the measures we have given would not be very large, nor even to this day prejudice the rest of mankind, or give them reason to complain or think themselves injured by this man's encroachment, though the race of men have now spread themselves to all the corners of the world and do infinitely exceed the smaller number [which] was at the beginning. Nay, the extent of ground is of so little value without labor that I have heard it affirmed that in Spain itself a man may be permitted

to plough, sow, and reap without being disturbed, upon land he has no other title to but only his making use of it. But on the contrary, the inhabitants think themselves beholden to him who by his industry on neglected and consequently waste land has increased the stock of corn which they wanted. But be this as it will, which I lay no stress on, this I dare boldly affirm, that the same rule of propriety . . . that every man should have as much as he could make use of would hold still in the world without straitening anybody, since there is land enough in the world to suffice double the inhabitants, had not the invention of money and the tacit agreement of men to put a value on it introduced (by consent) larger possessions and a right to them; which how it has done I shall by and by show more large.

37. This is certain, that in the beginning, before the desire of having more than men needed had altered the intrinsic value of things (which depends only on their usefulness to the life of man), or [men] had agreed that a little piece of yellow metal which would keep without wasting or decay should be worth a great piece of flesh or a whole heap of corn, though men had a right to appropriate by their labor each one to himself as much of the things of nature as he could use, yet this could not be much, nor to the prejudice of others where the same plenty was still left to those who would use the same industry. To which let me add that he who appropriates land to himself by his labor does not lessen but increase the common stock of mankind. For the provisions serving to the support of human life produced by one acre of enclosed and cultivated land are (to speak much within compass) ten times more than those which are yielded by an acre of land of an equal richness lying waste in common. And therefore he that encloses land and has a greater plenty of the conveniences of life from ten acres than he could have from an hundred left to nature may truly be said to give ninety acres to mankind. For his labor now supplies him with provisions out of ten acres which were but the product of an hundred lying in common. . . .

Before the appropriation of land, he who gathered as much of the wild fruit, killed, caught, or tamed as many of the beasts as he could —he that so employed his pains about any of the spontaneous products of nature as any way to alter them from the state which nature put them in by placing any of his labor on them—did thereby acquire a propriety in them: but if they perished in his possession without their due use, if the fruits rotted or the venison putrified before he could spend it, he offended against the common law of nature and was liable to be punished; he invaded his neighbor's share, for he had no right farther than his use called for any of them and they might serve to afford him conveniences of life.

38. The same measures governed the possession of land too: whatsoever he tilled and reaped, laid up and made use of before it spoiled, that was his peculiar right; whatsoever he enclosed and could feed and make use of, the cattle and product was also his. But if either the grass of his enclosure rotted on the ground or the fruit of his planting perished without gathering and laying up, his part of the earth, notwithstanding his enclosure, was still to be looked on as waste and might be the possession of any other. Thus at the beginning Cain might take as much ground as he could till and make it his own land, and yet leave enough to Abel's sheep to feed on; a few acres would serve for both their possessions. But as families increased and industry enlarged their stocks, their possessions enlarged with the need of them; but yet it was commonly without any fixed property in the ground they made use of, till they incorporated, settled themselves together and built cities; and then by consent they came in time to set out the bounds of their distinct territories, and agree on limits between them and their neighbors, and by laws within themselves settled the properties of those of the same society. For we see that in that part of the world which was first inhabited and therefore like to be best peopled, even as low down as Abraham's time they wandered with their flocks and their herds, which was their substance, freely up and down; and this Abraham did in a country where he was a stranger. Whence it is plain that at least a great part of the land lay in common. . . .

39. And thus without supposing any private dominion and property in Adam over all the world, exclusive of all other men—which can no way be proved nor by anyone's property be made out from it—but supposing the world given as it was to the children of men in common, we see how labor could make men distinct titles to several parcels of it for their private uses; wherein there could be no doubt of right, no room for quarrel.

40. Nor is it so strange as perhaps before consideration it may appear that the property of labor should be able to overbalance the community of land. For 'tis labor indeed that puts the difference of value on everything; and let anyone consider what the difference is between an acre of land planted with tobacco or sugar, sown with wheat or barley, and an acre of the same land lying in common without any husbandry upon it; and he will find that the improvement of labor makes the far greater part of the value. I think it will be but a very modest computation to say that of the products of the earth useful to the life of man 9/10 are the effects of labor. . . .

41. There cannot be a clearer demonstration of anything than several nations of Americans are of this, who are rich in land and poor in all the comforts of life—whom nature having furnished as liberally as any other people with the materials of plenty, i.e., a fruitful soil, apt to produce in abundance what might serve for food, raiment, and delight, yet for want of improving it by labor have not one hundredth part of the conveniences we enjoy, and a king of a large and fruitful territory there feeds, lodges, and is clad worse than a day laborer in England.

*   *   *

46. The greatest part of things really useful to the life of man . . . are generally things of short duration, such as if they are not consumed by use will decay and perish of themselves. Gold, silver, and diamonds are things that fancy or agreement hath put the value on more than real use and the necessary support of life. Now of those good things which nature hath provided in common, everyone had a right (as hath been said) to as much as he could use, and had a property in all that he could affect with his labor: all that his industry could extend to, to alter from the state nature had put it in, was his. He that gathered a hundred bushels of acorns or apples had thereby a property in them; they were his goods as soon as gathered. He was only to look that he used them before they spoiled; else he took more than his share and robbed others. And indeed it was a foolish thing, as well as dishonest, to hoard up more than he could make use of. If he gave away a part to anybody else, so that it perished not uselessly in his possession, these he also made use of. And if he also bartered away plums that would have rotted in a week for nuts that would last good for his eating a whole year, he did no injury; he wasted not the common stock, destroyed no part of the portion of goods that belonged to others, so long as nothing perished uselessly in his hands. Again, if he would give his nuts for a piece of metal, pleased with its color; or exchange his sheep for shells, or wool for a sparkling pebble or a diamond, and keep those by him all his life, he invaded not the right of others. He might heap up as much of these durable things as he pleased, the exceeding of the bounds of his just property not lying in the largeness of his possession, but the perishing of anything useless in it.

47. And thus came in the use of money, some lasting thing that men might keep without spoiling, and that by mutual consent men would take in exchange for the truly useful but perishable supports of life.

48. And as different degrees of industry were apt to give men pos-

sessions in different proportions, so this invention of money gave them the opportunity to continue and enlarge them. For supposing an island separate from all possible commerce with the rest of the world, wherein there were but a hundred families, but there were sheep, horses, and cows, with other useful animals, wholesome fruits, and land enough for corn for a hundred thousand times as many; but nothing in the island (either because of its commonness or perishableness) fit to supply the place of money: what reason could anyone have there to enlarge his possessions beyond the use of his family . . . ? Where there is not something both lasting and scarce, and so valuable to be hoarded up, there men will not be apt to enlarge their possessions of land were it never so rich, never so free for them to take. For I ask what would a man value ten thousand or an hundred thousand acres of excellent land, ready cultivated and well stocked too with cattle, in the middle of the inland parts of America, where he has no hopes of commerce with other parts of the world to draw money to him by the sale of the product? It would not be worth the enclosing, and we should see him give up again to the wild common of nature whatever was more than would supply the conveniences of life to be had there for him and his family.

49. Thus in the beginning all the world was America, and more so than that is now; for no such thing as money was anywhere known. Find out something that hath the use and value of money amongst his neighbours, [and] you shall see the same man will begin presently to enlarge his possessions.

50. But since gold and silver, being little useful to the life of man in proportion to food, raiment, and carriage, has its value only from the consent of man, whereof labor yet makes in great part the measure, it is plain that men have agreed to disproportionate and unequal possession of the earth, they having by a tacit and voluntary consent found out a way how a man may fairly possess more land than he himself can use the product of, by receiving in exchange for the overplus gold and silver, which may be hoarded up without injury to anyone, these metals not spoiling or decaying in the hands of the possessor. This partage of things in an inequality of private possessions men have made practicable out of the bounds of society and without compact, only by putting a value on gold and silver and tacitly agreeing in the use of money. For in governments the laws regulate the right of property, and the possession of land is determined by positive constitutions.

51. And thus, I think, it is very easy to conceive without any difficulty how labor could at first begin a title of property in the common things of nature and how the spending it upon our uses

bounded it—so that there could then be no reason of quarrelling about title nor any doubt about the largeness of possession it gave. Right and conveniency went together; for as a man had a right to all he could employ his labor upon, so he had no temptation to labor for more than he could make use of. This left no room for controversy about the title, nor for encroachment on the right of others; what portion a man carved to himself was easily seen; and it was useless as well as dishonest to carve himself too much or take more than he needed.

Political or Civil Society

From the *Second Treatise of Government*, chap. vii.

77. God, having made such a creature that in his own judgment it was not good for him to be alone, put him under strong obligations of necessity, convenience, and inclination to drive him into society; [and] as well fitted him with understanding and language to continue and enjoy it. The first society was between man and wife, which gave beginning to that between parents and children; to which, in time, that between master and servant came to be added. And though all these might and commonly did meet together and make up but one family, wherein the master or mistress of it had some sort of rule proper to a family, each of these or all together came short of political society; as we shall see if we consider the different ends, ties, and bounds of each of these.

78. Conjugal society is made by a voluntary compact between man and woman; and though it consists chiefly in such a communion and right in one another's bodies as is necessary to its chief end, procreation, yet it draws with it mutual support and assistance, and a communion of interest too, as necessary not only to unite their care and affection, but also necessary to their common offspring, who have a right to be nourished and maintained by them till they are able to provide for themselves.

79. For the end of conjunction between male and female being not barely procreation but the continuation of the species, this conjunction betwixt male and female ought to last even after procreation, so long as is necessary to the nourishment and support of the young ones, who are to be sustained by those that got them till they are able to shift and provide for themselves. This rule, which the infinite wise maker hath set to the works of his hands, we find the inferior

creatures steadily obey. In those viviparous animals which feed on grass the conjunction between male and female lasts no longer than the very act of copulation, because the teat of the dam being sufficient to nourish the young till it be able to feed on the grass, the male only begets, but concerns not himself for the female or young, to whose sustenance he can contribute nothing. But in beasts of prey the conjunction lasts longer, because the dam not being able well to subsist herself and nourish her numerous offspring by her own prey alone, a more laborious as well as more dangerous way of living than by feeding on grass, the assistance of the male is necessary to the maintenance of their common family, which cannot subsist till they are able to prey for themselves but by the joint care of male and female. . . .

80. And herein I think lies the chief if not the only reason why the male and female in mankind are tied to a longer conjunction than other creatures, *viz.,* because the female is capable of conceiving and *de facto* is commonly with child again and brings forth too a new birth long before the former is out of a dependency for support on his parents' help . . . whereby the father, who is bound to take care for these he hath begot, is under an obligation to continue in conjugal society with the same woman longer than other creatures.

*　　　*　　　*

85. Master and servant are names as old as history, but given to those of far different condition; for a free man makes himself a servant to another by selling him for a certain time the service he undertakes to do in exchange for wages he is to receive; and though this commonly puts him into the family of his master and under the ordinary discipline thereof, yet it gives the master but a temporary power over him, and no greater than what is contained in the contract between them. But there is another sort of servants, which by a peculiar name we call slaves, who, being captives taken in a just war, are by the right of nature subjected to the absolute dominion and arbitrary power of their masters. These men having, as I say, forfeited their lives and with it their liberties, and lost their estates, and being in the state of slavery not capable of any property, cannot in that state be considered as any part of civil society, the chief end whereof is the preservation of property.

86. Let us therefore consider a master of a family with all these subordinate relations of wife, children, servants, and slaves united under the domestic rule of a family; which what resemblance soever it may have in its order, offices, and number too, with a little commonwealth, yet is very far from it, both in its constitution, power,

and end: or if it must be thought a monarchy and the paterfamilias the absolute monarch in it, absolute monarchy will have but a very shattered and short power, when 'tis plain by what has been said before that the master of the family has a very distinct and differently limited power, both as to time and extent, over those several persons that are in it; for excepting the slave (and the family is as much a family and his power as paterfamilias as great, whether there be any slaves in his family or no) he has no legislative power of life and death over any of them, and none too but what a mistress of a family may have as well as he. And he certainly can have no absolute power over the whole family who has but a very limited one over every individual in it. But how a family or any other society of men differ from that which is properly political society we shall best see by considering wherein political society itself consists.

87. Man being born, as has been proved, with a title to perfect freedom and an uncontrolled enjoyment of all the rights and privileges of the law of nature equally with any other man or number of men in the world, hath by nature a power not only to preserve his property, that is, his life, liberty, and estate, against the injuries and attempts of other men, but to judge of and punish the breaches of that law in others, as he is persuaded the offence deserves, even with death. . . . But because no political society can be nor subsist without having in itself the power to preserve the property, and in order thereunto punish the offences, of all those of that society, there—and there only—is political society where every one of the members hath quitted this natural power, resigned it up into the hands of the community in all cases that exclude him not from appealing for protection to the law established by it. And thus all private judgment of every particular member being excluded, the community comes to be umpire by settled standing rules, indifferent and the same to all parties; and by men having authority from the community for the execution of those rules decides all the differences that may happen between any members of that society concerning any matter of right, and punishes those offences which any member hath committed against the society with such penalties as the law has established: whereby it is easy to discern who are and who are not in political society together. Those who are united into one body and have a common established law and judicature to appeal to, with authority to decide controversies between them and punish offenders, are in civil society one with another; but those who have no such common appeal—I mean on earth—are still in the state of nature, each being, where there is no other, judge for himself and executioner; which is, as I have before shown it, the perfect state of nature.

88. And thus the commonwealth comes by a power to set down what punishment shall belong to the several transgressions . . . committed amongst the members of that society (which is the power of making laws) as well as it has the power to punish any injury done unto any of its members by anyone that is not of it (which is the power of war and peace); and all this for the preservation of the property of all the members of that society, as far as is possible. . . .

89. Wherever therefore any number of men are so united into one society as to quit every one his executive power of the law of nature and to resign it to the public, there and there only is a political or civil society. And this is done wherever any number of men in the state of nature enter into society to make one people, one body politic under one supreme government, or else when anyone joins himself to and incorporates with any government already made. For hereby he authorizes the society or—which is all one—the legislative thereof, to make laws for him as the public good of the society shall require, to the execution whereof his own assistance (as to his own decrees) is due. And this puts men out of a state of nature into that of a commonwealth, by setting up a judge on earth with authority to determine all the controversies and redress the injuries that may happen to any member of the commonwealth, which judge is the legislative or magistrates appointed by it. And wherever there are any number of men however associated that have no such decisive power to appeal to, there they are still in the state of nature.

90. Hence it is evident that absolute monarchy, which by some men is counted the only government in the world, is indeed inconsistent with civil society and so can be no form of civil government at all. For the end of civil society being to avoid and remedy those inconveniences of the state of nature which necessarily follow from every man's being judge in his own case, by setting up a known authority to which everyone of that society may appeal upon any injury received or controversy that may arise, and which every one of the society ought to obey; wherever any persons are who have not an authority to appeal to for the decision of any difference between them, there those persons are still in the state of nature. And so is every absolute prince in respect of those who are under his dominion.

91. For he being supposed to have all, both legislative and executive, power in himself alone, there is no judge to be found; no appeal lies open to anyone who may fairly and indifferently and with authority decide, and from whose decision relief and redress may be expected of any injury or inconveniency that may be suffered from the prince or by his order: so that such a man however entitled, czar

or Grand Signior or how you please, is as much in the state of nature with all under his dominion as he is with the rest of mankind. For wherever any two men are who have no standing rule and common judge to appeal to on earth for the determination of controversies of right betwixt them, there they are still in the state of nature and under all the inconveniencies of it—with only this woeful difference to the subject, or rather slave, of an absolute prince: that whereas in the ordinary state of nature he has a liberty to judge of his right, and according to the best of his power to maintain it; now whenever his property is invaded by the will and order of his monarch, he has not only no appeal as those in society ought to have, but as if he were degraded from the common state of rational creatures, is denied a liberty to judge of or to defend his right, and so is exposed to all the misery and inconveniencies that man can fear from one who, being in the unrestrained state of nature, is yet corrupted with flattery and armed with power.

92. For he that thinks absolute power purifies men's bloods and corrects the baseness of human nature need read but the history of this or any other age to be convinced of the contrary. He that would have been insolent and injurious in the woods of America would not probably be much better in a throne, where perhaps learning and religion shall be found out to justify all that he shall do to his subjects and the sword presently silence all those that dare question it. For what the protection of absolute monarchy is, what kind of fathers of their countries it makes princes to be, and to what degree of happiness and security it carries civil society where this sort of government is grown to perfection, he that will look into the late relation of Ceylon may easily see.*

The Power of the Majority

From the *Second Treatise of Government*, chap. viii.

95. Men being, as has been said, by nature all free, equal, and independent, no one can be put out of this estate and subjected to the political power of another without his own consent. The only way whereby anyone divests himself of his natural liberty and puts

---

* *An Historical Relation of the Island of Ceylon*, by Robert Knox (1680). Locke's original readers in 1690 probably had a more immediate subject for reflection in the recently ended reign of James II.

on the bonds of civil society is by agreeing with other men to join and unite into a community for their comfortable, safe, and peaceable living one amongst another in a secure enjoyment of their properties and a greater security against any that are not of it. This any number of men may do, because it injures not the freedom of the rest; they are left as they were in the liberty of the state of nature. When any number of men have so consented to make one community or government, they are thereby presently incorporated and make one body politic, wherein the majority have a right to act and conclude the rest.

96. For when any number of men have by the consent of every individual made a community, they have thereby made that community one body with a power to act as one body, which is only by the will and determination of the majority. . . . It being necessary to that which is one body to move one way, it is necessary the body should move that way whither the greater force carries it, which is the consent of the majority; or else it is impossible it should act or continue one body, one community, which the consent of every individual that united into it agreed that it should; and so everyone is bound by that consent to be concluded by the majority. . . .

97. And thus every man, by consenting with others to make one body politic under one government, puts himself under an obligation to every one of that society to submit to the determination of the majority and to be concluded by it; or else this original compact whereby he with others incorporates into one society would signify nothing and be no compact if he be left free and under no other ties than he was in before in the state of nature. For what appearance would there be of any compact? What new engagement if he were no farther tied by any decrees of the society than he himself thought fit and did actually consent to? This would be still as great a liberty as he himself had before his compact or anyone else in the state of nature hath, who may submit himself and consent to any acts of it if he thinks fit.

98. For if the consent of the majority shall not in reason be received as the act of the whole and conclude every individual, nothing but the consent of every individual can make anything to be the act of the whole: but such a consent is next impossible ever to be had if we consider the infirmities of health and avocations of business, which . . . will necessarily keep many away from the public assembly. To which if we add the variety of opinions and contrariety of interests which unavoidably happen in all collections of men, the coming into society upon such terms would be only like Cato's coming into the theatre only to go out again. Such a constitution as this

would make the mighty Leviathan of a shorter duration than the feeblest creatures and not let it outlast the day it was born in; which cannot be supposed till we can think that rational creatures should desire and constitute societies only to be dissolved. . . .

The Dissolution of Government

From the *Second Treatise of Government,* chap. xix.

211. He that will with any clearance speak of the dissolution of government ought in the first place to distinguish between the dissolution of the society and the dissolution of the government. That which makes the community and brings men out of the loose state of nature into one politic society is the agreement which everyone has with the rest to incorporate and act as one body and so be one distinct commonwealth. The usual and almost only way whereby this union is dissolved is the inroad of foreign force making a conquest upon them. For in that case (not being able to maintain and support themselves as one entire and independent body) the union belonging to that body which consisted therein must necessarily cease and so everyone return to the state he was in before, with a liberty to shift for himself and provide for his own safety as he thinks fit in some other society. Whenever the society is dissolved, 'tis certain the government of that society cannot remain. Thus conquerors' swords often cut up governments by the roots and mangle societies to pieces, separating the subdued or scattered multitude from the protection of and dependence on that society which ought to have preserved them from violence. . . .

212. Besides this overturning from without, governments are dissolved from within.

First, when the legislative is altered. Civil society being a state of peace amongst those who are of it, from whom the state of war is excluded by the umpirage which they have provided in their legislative for the ending all differences that may arise amongst any of them, 'tis in their legislative that the members of a commonwealth are united and combined together into one coherent living body. This is the soul that gives form, life, and unity to the commonwealth; from hence the several members have their mutual influence, sympathy, and connection; and therefore when the legislative is broken or dissolved, dissolution and death follows. . . .

When any one or more shall take upon them to make laws whom the people have not appointed so to do, they make laws without authority, which the people are not therefore bound to obey; by which means they come again to be out of subjection and may constitute to themselves a new legislative as they think best, being in full liberty to resist the force of those who without authority would impose anything upon them.

* * *

221. There is . . . secondly, another way whereby governments are dissolved, and that is when the legislative or the prince either of them act contrary to their trust.

First the legislative acts against the trust reposed in them when they endeavor to invade the property of the subject and to make themselves or any part of the community masters or arbitrary disposers of the lives, liberties, or fortunes of the people.

222. The reason why men enter into society is the preservation of their property; and the end why they choose and authorize a legislative is that there may be laws made and rules set as guards and fences to the properties of all the members of the society to limit the power and moderate the dominion of every part and member of the society. For since it can never be supposed to be the will of the society that the legislative should have a power to destroy that which everyone designs to secure by entering into society and for which the people submitted themselves to the legislators of their own making, whenever the legislators endeavor to take away and destroy the property of the people or to reduce them to slavery under arbitrary power, they put themselves into a state of war with the people, who are thereupon absolved from any further obedience and are left to the common refuge which God hath provided for all men against force and violence. Whensoever therefore the legislative shall transgress this fundamental rule of society, and either by ambition, fear, folly, or corruption endeavor to grasp themselves—or put into the hands of any other—an absolute power over the lives, liberties, and estates of the people, by this breach of trust they forfeit the power the people had put into their hands for quite contrary ends; and it devolves to the people, who have a right to resume their orginal liberty and by the establishment of a new legislative (such as they shall think fit) provide for their own safety and security, which is the end for which they are in society. What I have said here concerning the legislative in general holds true also concerning the supreme executor, who having a double trust put in him, both to have a part in the legislative and the supreme execution of the law, acts against both

when he goes about to set up his own arbitrary will as the law of the society. He acts also contrary to his trust when he either employs the force, treasure, and offices of the society to corrupt the representatives and gain them to his purposes; or openly pre-engages the electors and prescribes to their choice such whom he has by solicitations, threats, promises, or otherwise won to his designs and employs them to bring in such who have promised beforehand what to vote and what to enact. Thus to regulate candidates and electors and new model the ways of election, what is it but to cut up the government by the roots and poison the very fountain of public security? For the people, having reserved to themselves the choice of their representatives as the fence to their properties, could do it for no other end but that they might always be freely chosen and, so chosen, freely act and advise as the necessity of the commonwealth and the public good should upon examination and mature debate be judged to require. This, those who give their votes before they hear the debate and have weighed the reasons on all sides are not capable of doing. . . .

223. To this perhaps it will be said that, the people being ignorant and always discontented, to lay the foundation of government in the unsteady opinion and uncertain humor of the people is to expose it to certain ruin; and no government will be able long to subsist if the people may set up a new legislative whenever they take offence at the old one. To this I answer: quite the contrary. People are not so easily got out of their old forms as some are apt to suggest. They are hardly to be prevailed with to amend the acknowledged faults in the frame they have been accustomed to. And if there be any original defects or adventitious ones introduced by time or corruption, 'tis not an easy thing to get them changed even when all the world sees there is an opportunity for it. This slowness and aversion in the people to quit their old constitutions has, in the many revolutions which have been seen in this kingdom, in this and former ages, still kept us to—or after some interval of fruitless attempts still brought us back again to—our old legislative of king, lords, and commons: and whatever provocations have made the crown be taken from some of our princes' heads, they never carried the people so far as to place it in another line.

224. But 'twill be said this hypothesis lays a ferment for frequent rebellion. To which I answer:

First, no more than any other hypothesis. For when the people are made miserable and find themselves exposed to the ill usage of arbitrary power, cry up their governors as much as you will for sons of Jupiter, let them be sacred and divine, descended or authorized from heaven, give them out for whom or what you please: the same will happen. The people generally ill treated . . . will be ready upon any occasion to ease themselves of a burden that sits heavy upon them. They will wish and seek for the opportunity which, in the change, weakness, and accidents of human affairs, seldom delays long to offer itself. He must have lived but a little while in the world who has not seen examples of this in his time; and he must have read very little who cannot produce examples of it in all sorts of governments in the world.

225. Secondly, I answer such revolutions happen not upon every little mismanagement in public affairs. Great mistakes in the ruling part, many wrong and inconvenient laws, and all the slips of human frailty will be borne by the people without mutiny or murmur. But if a long train of abuses, prevarications, and artifices all tending the same way make the design visible to the people, and they cannot but feel what they lie under and see whither they are going, 'tis not to be wondered that they should then rouse themselves and endeavor to put the rule into such hands which may secure to them the ends for which government was at first erected. . . .

*   *   *

228. But if they who say it lays a foundation for rebellion mean that it may occasion civil wars or intestine broils to tell the people they are absolved from obedience when illegal attempts are made upon their liberties or properties, and may oppose the unlawful violence of those who were their magistrates when they invade their properties contrary to the trust put in them, and that therefore this doctrine is not to be allowed, being so destructive to the peace of the world, they may as well say upon the same ground that honest men may not oppose robbers or pirates because this may occasion disorder or bloodshed. If any mischief come in such cases, it is not to be charged upon him who defends his own right, but on him that invades his neighbor's. If the innocent honest man must quietly quit all he has for peaces's sake to him who will lay violent hands upon it, I desire it may be considered what kind of peace there will be in the world which consists only in violence and rapine and which is to be maintained only for the benefit of robbers and oppressors. . . . Polyphemus's den gives us a perfect pattern of such a peace and such a government, wherein Ulysses and his companions had nothing to do but quietly to suffer themselves to be devoured. And no doubt Ulysses, who was a prudent man, preached up passive obedience and exhorted them to a quiet submission by representing to them of what concernment peace was to mankind, and by showing the in-

conveniencies might happen if they should offer to resist Polyphemus who had now the power over them.

229. The end of government is the good of mankind; and which is best for mankind, that the people should be always exposed to the boundless will of tyranny, or that the rulers should be sometimes liable to be opposed when they grow exorbitant in the use of their power and employ it for the destruction and not the preservation of the properties of their people?

Part VIII

DEFENDERS OF THE FAITH

Introduction

Judged by purely quantitative standards, the seventeenth century was still deeply Christian. Books on religious subjects probably outnumbered those devoted to all other topics put together. The production of sermons alone took the sort of time and money that we are accustomed to lavish on scientific research. Besides these purely devotional writings there was an unabated tide of religious polemic, carrying on the now hereditary quarrels of the Reformation as well as the new internecine disputes between Jesuit and Jansenist or Arminian and Calvinist. Finally, religion was so intimately linked with science and politics that almost every selection in this book could be considered part of religious thought.

But purely quantitative standards are of course inadequate: it does not take much reading to see that the Christianity of the seventeenth century was an embattled and even defensive faith. For the first time we can identify substantial numbers of what might be called religious liberals: deists and Socinians who had ceased to believe in such "mysterious" and "unreasonable" doctrines as sin and redemption, and even Unitarians who, like their famous Boston descendants, believed in one God, at most. There were now outright freethinkers or atheists—by one famous if probably exaggerated estimate, fifty thousand of them in and near Paris alone.

Such a general denial of the fundamental tenets of the faith had not been seen in Christendom since the fifth century, and naturally it called for the most energetic rebuttal that could be arranged. The traditional philosophical arguments for the existence of God were refurbished by Descartes and Newton, among others. Though Descartes was probably sincere in believing that his demonstration of the existence of God would buttress the Catholic faith to which he had always remained loyal, and indeed was disappointed when his philosophy encountered opposition in ecclesiastical circles, Bossuet was quite correct in seeing that Cartesianism was having a profoundly unsettling effect on faith (p. 148). Henry More, a Cambridge Platonist, had been one of Descartes' earliest admirers in England, but by 1671 he was expressing no surprise that there were many in Holland "mere scoffers at religion, and atheistical, that professed themselves Cartesians." He claimed always to have seen "how prejudicial Descartes' mechanical pretensions are to the belief of a God." *

Descartes' attempted vindication of Christianity was not the only philosophical weapon which turned out to have a double edge. Catholic intellectuals, especially in France, often pressed the attack against unbelief by taking a position of extreme skepticism. Theology was not alone in being unverifiable by the unaided reason, they argued; once we realize the dubiousness of everything that is conventionally taken to be certain, we shall see that there is no basis for a distinction between faith and knowledge. "Fideism," as this position was called, drew heavily on Montaigne's *Essays* (1580-88). Notwithstanding its frequent use as an argument for Catholicism, it is nevertheless a heresy—in fact, the only original heresy of modern times. The orthodox Catholic position is that the unaided reason can reach some, though not all, truths about God; and for undermining this position Montaigne's essays were, late in the seventeenth century, put on the Index.

Christianity suffered more self-inflicted wounds in the ceaseless efforts of Protestants and Catholics to discredit each other, since both were only too eager to press into service arguments which discredited Christianity almost as much. Most of the case which the *philosophes* were to make in the subsequent century was already found in Bayle's *Dictionary,* and Bayle had taken his choicest examples of the knavery of priests from the polemical writings of other priests. The writing of church history was sometimes nothing but an excuse for muckraking of this character. Another excellent example of scholarship which undermines in the process of defense is Simon's Biblical criticism (page 151). Simon, a Catholic priest, believed—or pretended to believe—that his demonstration that the text of the Bible had been corrupted beyond repair could only drive Protestants back to the infallibility of Church tradition; but this did not prevent his punishment by his ecclesiastical superiors and the confiscation of the first edition of his work.

* Henry More to Robert Boyle in Boyle, *Works* (London, 1772), VI, p. 514.

Ironically, therefore, the chief task of an effective seventeenth-century defender of Christianity was first to fight off his fellow defenders. Since not many men have thought themselves into being true Christians, a mere reasoned demonstration of God's existence would not suffice. Seventeenth-century apologetics rightly based the case for Christianity on the process by which men felt their lives transformed. Here a Cambridge Platonist like John Smith came very close to a Quaker who believed that there was no point in going to Cambridge (pages 150 and 151). Religious experience was indeed for the Quakers the solution of any difficulties about the textual purity of the Bible; one of them describes the experience of being possessed by the spirit of God as "giving experimental knowledge of what is recorded in Acts ii, 37."

The authenticity of religious experience also lies at the heart of the great unfinished defense of Christianity that we know as Pascal's *Pensées*. This is not always easy to see, since there are a great many subjects treated in the *Pensées*—partly because it was compiled from all the papers found in Pascal's study after his death,* and partly because Pascal was one of the universal geniuses of his or any age, whose remarkable range of interests was naturally reflected in his writings. But the book gains a certain unity if seen as a set of meditations on certain recurring themes—infinity, probability, custom, miracles, sacred history (both Jewish and Christian), and the greatness and misery of man.

To Pascal the great achievements of reason and science in his own day—to which he himself had contributed so much—did not alleviate the fundamental misery (we would now say 'absurdity") of the human condition. Man is the creature who would play the angel, but must play the beast; the animal who can never grasp the infinite, yet can never be content with the finite. Since the infinite is beyond him, there is no point in dreaming of a method by which uncertainty (and thus the necessity for choice or calculation of probabilities) would be permanently eliminated. In short, reason will never solve our moral problems; we must bet.

Once we accept the inevitability of uncertainty, we will cease to disregard our own history or that of the human race. Pascal was not

* The papers subsequently published as the *Pensées* were probably intended for different books. We cannot be sure which would have been included in his projected apology for Christianity, or in what order. Fortunately the abrupt changes of subject and fragmentary form of the *Pensées* brilliantly suit the epigrammatic cast of Pascal's mind, but it does make a considerable difference in what order the separate "thoughts" are read. (I have followed the order and enumeration recently established by Louis Lafuma, which is based on the original "Copie" of Pascal's papers.)

willing to ignore history simply because it did not readily conform to the simple reasonings of a man of good sense. While he consistently avoids all philosophical arguments that God exists, he argues that Christianity can be proved to be divine just because of its persistence through time despite its hostility to all our passions. Whereas rationalists were fond of appealing from custom to nature, Pascal responded that nature was only first custom: man has no "nature" or essence which can be taken out of the flow of history. Indeed, the man who wants to become a Christian should not pile up arguments, but instead force himself to adopt the habits of the Christian life and thus submit his reason to the force of sheer repetitive, unreflective experience.

Perhaps we can understand the value that Pascal put on experience if we turn from the papers found on his desk to the one found sewn into his clothing: the "Memorial" (page 166) which he never intended that we should see. There he describes the experiences of a November evening perhaps something like that one in Descartes' life a quarter-century earlier, and yet completely different: for his experience led Pascal, as he wished to lead others, to the God not of the philosophers but of Abraham, Isaac, and Jacob—the true God of men.

Cartesianism Will Bring Hatred against the Dogmas of the Church

From a letter of Bossuet to a disciple of Malebranche (1687) in Paul Hazard, *La crise de la conscience européene* (Paris: Voivin, 1935), I, pp. 285-286. Translated from French.

From these principles, imperfectly understood, another idea, entailing the gravest consequences, imperceptibly gains possession of men's minds. For, on the ground that we ought to assent only to what we perfectly understand—which, within limits, is perfectly true—everyone takes the liberty to say: "I understand this; and I do not understand that"; and on this basis alone he accepts or rejects anything he likes, forgetting that, besides our own clear and definite ideas, there are other confused and general ideas which nevertheless contain truths so essential that to deny them would be to reduce everything to chaos. On this pretext he brings in a liberty of judgment which makes him disregard Tradition and rashly put forward whatever he personally may happen to think.

*   *   *

I see . . . preparations for a great battle against the Church in the name of Cartesian philosophy. I see more than one heresy issuing from the womb of that philosophy and its principles—to my mind imperfectly understood—and I foresee that consequences drawn from it contrary to the dogmas our fathers held will make the Church seem odious, depriving her of the fruit she was entitled to expect from them in establishing in the minds of philosophers a firm belief in the divinity and immortality of the soul.

Newton States the Argument from Design

From a letter of Newton to Richard Bentley (1692) in Newton, *Complete Works* (London, 1782), IV, pp. 429-430.

When I wrote my treatise about our system,* I had an eye upon such principles as might work with considering men for the belief of a Deity; and nothing can rejoice me more than to find it useful for that purpose. But if I have done the public any service this way, it is due to nothing but industry and patient thought.

As to your first query, it seems to me that if the matter of our sun and planets and all the matter of the universe were evenly scattered throughout all the heavens, and every particle had an innate gravity towards all the rest, and the whole space throughout which this matter was scattered was but finite, the matter on the outside of this space would by its gravity tend towards all the matter on the inside and by consequence fall down into the middle of the whole space and there compose one great spherical mass. But if the matter was evenly disposed throughout an infinite space, it could never convene into one mass; but some of it would convene into one mass and some into another, so as to make an infinite number of great masses, scattered at great distances from one to another throughout all that infinite space. And thus might the sun and fixed stars be formed, supposing the matter were of a lucid nature. But how matter should divide itself into two sorts, and that part of it which is fit to compose

* *Mathematical Principles of Natural Philosophy.*

a shining body should fall down into one mass and make a sun, and the rest which is fit to compose an opaque body should coalesce, not into one great body like the shining matter, but into many little ones; or if the sun at first were an opaque body like the planets or the planets lucid bodies like the sun, how he alone should be changed into a shining body whilst all they continue opaque, or all they be changed into opaque ones whilst he remains unchanged, I do not think explicable by mere natural causes but am forced to ascribe it to the counsel and contrivance of a voluntary Agent.

Experimental Religion

From George Fox, *Journal* (London, 1694), I, p. 8.

Now after I had received that opening from the Lord, that to be bred at Oxford or Cambridge was not sufficient to fit a man to be a minister of Christ, I regarded the priests* less and looked more after the dissenting people. . . . But as I had forsaken all the priests, so I left the separate preachers also . . . for I saw there was none among them all that could speak to my condition. And when all my hopes in them and in all men was gone** so that I had nothing outwardly to help me nor could tell me what to do, then O! I heard a voice which said, "There is one, even Christ Jesus, that can speak to thy Condition." And when I heard it my heart did leap for joy. Then the Lord did let me see why there was none upon the earth that could speak to my condition—namely, that I might give him all the glory. . . . And this I knew experimentally.

Empirical Religion

From John Smith, "Concerning the True Way or Method of Attaining to Divine Knowledge," in *Discourses* (London, 1660), pp. 1-4.

Were I indeed to define divinity, I should rather call it a divine life than a divine science, it being something rather to be

---

* Ministers of the established church. At this time these were Presbyterians for the most part, while the "dissenting" or "separate" people were Congregationalists and Baptists.

** This experience happened to Fox in 1647.

understood by a spiritual sensation than by any verbal description.

＊   ＊   ＊

To seek our divinity merely in books and writings is to seek the living among the dead; we do but in vain seek God many times in these, where his truth too often is not so much enshrined as entombed. No; *intra te quaere Deum,* seek for God within thine own soul; he is best discerned νοερᾷ ἐπαφῇ, as Plotinus phraseth it, by an intellectual touch of him: we must see with our eyes, and hear with our ears, and with our hands must handle the word of life. . . . David, when he would teach us how to know what the divine goodness is, calls not for speculation but sensation: "Taste and see how good the Lord is."

＊   ＊   ＊

It is but a thin, airy knowledge that is got by mere speculation, which is ushered in by syllogisms and demonstrations; but that which springs forth from true goodness . . . brings such a divine light into the soul as is more clear and convincing than any demonstration. The reason why—notwithstanding all our acute reasons and subtle disputes—truth prevails no more in the world is we so often disjoin truth and true goodness, which in themselves can never be disunited. . . .

The Text of the Bible Hopelessly Corrupt

From the Preface to Richard Simon, *Critical History of the Old Testament* (Paris, 1678). Translated from French.

I have shown that the Hebrews were not very polished writers; that they habitually got things out of order and repeated the same things; and that they frequently had scarcely begun on one subject before skipping suddenly to another, and then resuming their original one. (It is easy to recognize this style in the books of the New Testament, especially in the Epistles of St. Paul.) But since it would be difficult to justify all the transpositions and repetitions that are found in the books of Moses by the manner in which they were accustomed to express themselves, I have been obliged to have recourse to other rules—leaving everyone the liberty, however, to believe what he pleases, since these are matters which we can be ignorant of, and even speak freely of, without doing any wrong to religion. As St. Augustine says, "in which things—saving our faith as Christians—we can either remain ignorant of the truth and suspend definitive judgment, or else throw suspicion on what is human and infirm." *

. . . The great changes which have happened to the copies of the Bible since the first originals were lost (as we have shown in the first book of this work) entirely destroy the basis of Protestantism and Socinianism, since they only consult these same copies of the Bible as they exist today. If the truths of religion had not been confided to the Church, it would not be safe to search for them now in books which have been subject to so many changes and which have depended in so many things on the will of the copyists.

The Apology for the Christian Religion

From Pascal, *Pensées* (Paris, 1670). Translated from the French text established by Louis Lafuma (Paris: Éditions du Seuil, 1962).

12. Men despise religion. They hate it and fear that it might be true. To cure this it is necessary to begin by showing that religion is not contrary to reason, [and] venerable, by inspiring respect for it. Then to make it attractive; to make good men hope that it is true, and then show that it is true.

Venerable, because it has thorough knowledge of the human condition. Attractive, because it promises the true good.

51. "Why do you kill me to benefit yourself? I am not armed."

"What! Do you not live on the other side of the water? My friend, if you lived on this side I would be a murderer, and it would be unjust to kill you like that. But since you live on the other side, I am a brave man and it is just."

60. On what will man found the order of the world which he wishes to govern? Will it be on the caprice of each individual? What confusion! Will it be on justice? He is ignorant of it. Certainly if he did know it he would not have established the maxim—more widespread than any other among men—that each should follow the cus-

---

* In Latin in the original.

toms of his own region. The brilliance of any true equity would have captivated all nations, and legislators would not have taken for their models the whims and fantasies of the Persians and Germans instead of this immutable justice. We should have seen justice firmly implanted in all the states of the world and in all ages; whereas we see neither justice nor injustice which does not change its quality with a change of climate. Three degrees of latitude reverses all of jurisprudence; a meridian decides what is truth. After a few years of possession, fundamental laws change. Right is subject to seasons; the entrance of Saturn into Leo marks the beginning of such and such a crime. An absurd justice which is bounded by a river! Truth this side of the Pyrenees, error on that side.

Men admit that justice does not consist in these customs, but claim that it resides in the natural laws which are common to all nations. Certainly they would maintain their position stubbornly if we could meet with, in all the random chaos in which human laws are distributed, even one which is universal. But such is the strangeness of this hodgepodge that there are none.

Theft, incest, the murder of children and of fathers—all have been reckoned virtuous actions. Can there be anything so absurd as that a man has the right to kill me because he lives on that side of the water and his prince has a quarrel with mine, even though I have none with him?

No doubt there are natural laws, but our fine corrupt reason has corrupted them all. "Nothing is our own anymore; what we call ours is only by convention." [Cicero] "Crimes are committed by act of the senate and by plebiscite." [Seneca] "Once we suffered from our vices; now from our laws." [Tacitus] * From this confusion it happens that one says that the essence of justice is the authority of the legislator; another, the convenience of the sovereign; another, present custom, and that this is the most certain. If we look to reason alone, there is no essential justice; everything moves with the times, like a pendulum. Custom is the whole of equity purely because it is in use. This is the mystical foundation of its authority. Whoever traces it back to its first principles destroys it. Nothing is so defective as these laws which remedy defects. Whoever obeys them because they are just obeys an imaginary justice, not the essence of the law. Law is entirely self-contained; it is law and nothing more. He who would examine the motive for it will find it so weak and so slight that, if he is not accustomed to contemplating the prodigies of the human imagina-

* In Latin in the original. All three are quoted in Montaigne's essay "In Defense of Raymond Sebonde."

tion, he will marvel that a mere century has vested it with so much pomp and reverence. The art of factious opposition and of revolution lies in shaking the established customs by probing into their sources, in order to show their lack of authority and justice. We must return (they say) to the primitive and fundamental laws of the state, which unjust custom has abolished. This game is sure to lead to utter ruin; nothing will be just if weighed in this balance. . . .

114. The greatness of man is great in that he knows himself to be miserable; a tree does not know itself to be miserable. . . .

125. What are our natural principles, if not our customary principles? And, in children, those which they have received from the habits of their fathers, just as animals are taught to hunt?

A different custom would give them other principles. . . .

126. Fathers fear that the natural love of their children may wear out. What is this nature which nevertheless is subject to decay?

Custom is a second nature which destroys the first. But what is nature? why is custom not natural? I very much fear that this nature is nothing itself but first custom, as custom is second nature.

130.   If he vaunts himself, I shall humiliate him.
       If he humbles himself, I shall exalt him.
       And always contradict him.
       Until he comprehends
       that he is an incomprehensible freak of nature.

136. DIVERSIONS

When I occasionally ponder the various excitements of men and the pains and perils to which they expose themselves at Court or at war, which gives rise to so many quarrels and passions and desperate, often evil, enterprises, etc., I have often said that all the unhappiness of men comes from one simple thing: that they cannot remain quietly in one room. A man who has enough on which to live, if he knew how to stay happily at home, would not leave to go to sea or to the siege of some place. We pay such great sums for a commission in the army only because we find it intolerable never to budge from the town where we live; we only seek conversation and the diversions of gambling because we cannot live contentedly at home, etc.

But when I have considered more closely, when after having found the cause of all our misfortunes I have wished to discover the reasons for it, I have discovered that there is in effect only one, which consists in the natural wretchedness of our condition—weak and mortal, so miserable that nothing can console us when we think closely about it.

Of all conditions which we can imagine, endowed with all the good things which it is possible to possess, royalty is the finest; but let us imagine a king surrounded by everything which can satisfy him. If he is without diversions and is left to consider and reflect on what he is, his languishing happiness will not endure. He will necessarily fall a prey to premonitions of potential revolutions and finally of inevitable sickness and death—so that without what we call diversions he will be miserable, more miserable than the least of his subjects who plays and amuses himself.

This explains why gambling, the society of women, war, and high office are so sought after. It is not that there is in fact any happiness in them; nor can one imagine true happiness in the money that one might win in gambling or in the hare that one hunts. We would not want them if they were offered us as a gift. We do not desire a soft and peaceable way of life which allows us to think of our miserable condition; nor the dangers of war, nor the toils of office; but worrying about them diverts our attention from our condition and amuses us. (The reason why we prefer the chase to the capture.)

Hence men are so fond of noise and bustle. Hence prison is such dreadful punishment, and the pleasures of solitude so little understood. In fact, the greatest source of pleasure in the condition of kings is that people never stop trying to amuse them and procure for them all sorts of pleasures. The king is surrounded by people who think only of diverting him and preventing him from thinking of himself. For if he should think of himself, king though he be, he is wretched.

So this is all that men have been able to invent to make themselves happy! And those who pose as philosophers on this matter, and who believe that men are highly unreasonable to spend the day in running after a hare that they would not want to have bought, know little of our nature. This hare does not protect us from the prospect of death and the miseries which keep our minds off it; but the chase does protect us.

*   *   *

Thus runs our life away: we seek repose in surmounting various obstacles, and when we have surmounted them repose becomes intolerable because of the ennui which arises from it. We must abandon it and go looking for excitement.

For our minds are possessed either by the miseries which we have or by the ones which threaten us. And even if we think ourselves safe on every side, ennui would spring up of its own accord in the recesses of the heart where it has its natural roots and fill the mind with its venom.

Thus man is so wretched that he becomes bored even without any cause, merely from the state of his own nature. And he is so frivolous that even if he is full of a thousand essential causes for boredom the slightest thing, like a billiard table and a ball to shoot, is enough to amuse him.

But, will you say, what object has he in all this? One will boast tomorrow to his friends that he has played better than another. Others will sweat in their studies to show the learned that they have solved an algebra problem which has never been solved before; many others will expose themselves to extreme peril in order to boast later —just as foolishly, in my opinion—of some place which they have taken. And finally still others wear out their lives in studying these things, not to become more wise from them, but only to show off their knowledge. These last are the most foolish of the lot, since they are knowingly so, whereas we might think that the others would not be so foolish if they knew what they were doing.

Such a fool passes his life without boredom by gambling every day for some trifle. Give him every morning the money that he could win, on condition that he not gamble for it, and you make him unhappy. Perhaps you will say that he plays just for the amusement of the game and not for the stakes. Very well, make him play for nothing; he will not get excited and will be bored. Thus it is not simply the amusement which he seeks. A languid game without passion will be tedious; he must become excited about it and delude himself by imagining that he will be happy if he can win what he would have refused as a gift on condition of not playing for it. He needs to make for himself an object of passion which will excite his wrath, his desire, and his fear, in order to gain his imaginary end—very much like children who are frightened by the face which they themselves have painted up.

How does it happen that this man, who a few months ago lost his only son and who this morning was overwhelmed with quarrels and law-suits, now thinks no more of these things? Do not be amazed; he is completely absorbed in seeing where the boar that his dogs have

been so hotly pursuing for six hours will go. He needs nothing more.
Man, no matter how full of grief, will at once be happy for so long
as you can prevail on him to take up some diversion—and no matter
how happy he is, if not diverted or occupied by some passion or
amusement which prevents boredom from spreading, he will at once
be troubled and unhappy. . . .

173. If we submit everything to reason our religion will have nothing mysterious and supernatural.

If we flout the principles of reason our religion will be absurd and
ridiculous.

189. GOD THROUGH JESUS CHRIST

We know God only through Jesus Christ. Without this
mediator all communication with God is cut off. Through Jesus
Christ we know God. All those who have claimed to know God and
to prove his existence without Jesus Christ have only impotent
proofs. But to prove Jesus Christ we have the prophecies, which are
solid and palpable proofs. And these prophecies being accomplished
and proved true by the event give evidence of the certainty of these
truths; and hence they prove the divinity of Jesus Christ. . . . Apart
from him and without the scriptures, without original sin, without
the necessary mediator foretold and come, we cannot absolutely
prove God's existence, nor teach either good doctrine or good morals. But through Jesus Christ and in Jesus Christ we prove God and
teach morals and doctrine. Jesus Christ is thus the true God of
men.

But at the same time we know our misery, for this very God is
nothing else than the repairer of our misery. Thus we can only know
God well in knowing our sins.

Thus those who have known God without knowing their misery
have not glorified him, but have glorified themselves. "Because [the
world] knew not through wisdom, it pleased God to give salvation
through the foolishness of preaching." [I Corinthians i, 21]

192.   Knowledge of God without that of our misery gives rise to
         pride.
       Knowledge of our misery without that of God gives rise to
         despair.
       Knowledge of Jesus Christ is the happy medium, because
         there we find both God and our misery.

199. DISPROPORTION OF MAN

Let man contemplate the whole of nature in its full and lofty majesty. Let him put far from him the sight of those base objects which surround him. Let him look into this dazzling light set like an eternal lamp to illumine the universe, so that the earth appears to him like a point in the vast circuit which this star describes, and let him marvel that this vast circuit itself is only a very fine point compared to that which is traced by the stars which wheel in the firmament. But if our vision stops here, let our imagination pass beyond; it will fail to form conceptions well before nature fails to furnish material for them.

The entire visible universe is only an imperceptible flash in the broad bosom of nature. No idea can approach it. We may well inflate our conceptions beyond all conceivable space; we give birth only to atoms in comparison with the reality of things. The universe is an infinite sphere whose center is everywhere, whose circumference nowhere. In fact it is the greatest perceptible mark of the omnipotence of God that our imagination loses itself in this thought.

Now let man return to himself and consider what he is in relation to all that is. Let him see himself as lost; and from this tiny cell where he finds himself confined—I mean the universe—he will learn to value the earth, realms, cities, houses, and himself at their true worth.

What is a man in this infinity?

But now let us confront him with another prodigy, equally astonishing. Let him examine his knowledge of the smallest things. A cheese-mite offers him in the minuteness of its body particles incomparably smaller: the legs with their joints, the veins in the legs, the blood in the veins, the humors in the blood, the droplets in the humors, the vapors in the droplets. In thus subdividing these last things again he will exhaust his powers in these thoughts; and the last object at which he can arrive will now be the subject of our discourse. Perhaps he will think he has reached the smallest thing in nature.

I would make him see that therein lies a new abyss. I will paint for him not only the visible universe, but also the immensity of nature that we can conceive within the confines of this microcosm of the atom, so that he will see therein an infinite number of universes, each of which has its firmament, its planets, its earth—on the same scale as in the visible world—its animals on its earth, and finally even its cheese-mites, in which he will find again all that he found in the first, and thus the same thing again in endless, relentless procession, so that he will lose himself in these marvels, as astounding in their smallness as the others were in their vastness. For who will not marvel that our body, which a little while ago was not even perceptible in our universe—which is itself imperceptible in the bosom of the infinite—should now be a colossus, a world, or rather a universe in comparison to the nothingness which lies beyond our reach. Whoever regards himself in this fashion will be frightened of himself; and, bearing in mind that he is sustained in the mass which nature has given him between the two abysses of infinity and nothingness, he will tremble at the sight of these marvels. I believe that his curiosity will be changed to awe, and he will be more disposed to contemplate in silence than to inquire with presumption.

For, finally, what is man in nature? A nothingness compared to the infinite, and all compared to nothingness; a mean between nothing and everything, infinitely removed from understanding these extremes. The ends and principles of things are insuperably hidden from him in an impenetrable secret.

* * *

Let us then know our limitations. We are something, and we are not everything. Such existence as we have conceals from us the knowledge of those first beginnings which are born of nothingness; yet the littleness of our existence hides the vision of the infinite from us.

Our intellect holds the same place in the order of intelligible things that our body holds in the realm of nature.

Limited in every way, we find all our powers in a state which is a mean between two extremes. Our senses can perceive nothing extreme: too much noise deafens us; too much light dazzles us; we cannot see too far away or too close. Laconic and prolix speech are equally obscure. Too much truth astonishes us. . . . First principles are too obvious for us. Too much pleasure is inconvenient; we are displeased by music which is too harmonious; and a surfeit of benefits irritates us. . . . We feel neither extreme heat nor extreme cold. Excessive qualities are enemies to our senses; we suffer them without feeling them. . . .

In short, the extremes are things which might as well not exist for us or we for them; they escape us, or we them.

This is our true condition. It is this which makes us incapable of absolute knowledge or of absolute ignorance. We drift in a vast mediocrity, always floating and uncertain, pushed from one end to the other. When we think we have reached a point where we can settle down and establish ourselves, it swings away from us; and if we follow it, it escapes our grasp, slips away and vanishes forever. Nothing stays still for us. This is the condition which is natural to us—and yet that which is most contrary to our inclinations. We burn with desire to find a stable position and a final constant foundation on which to build a tower stretching up to the infinite; but our whole foundation cracks and an abyss yawns in the earth beneath us.

Consequently, let us not seek stability and security; our reason is always deceived by the inconstancy of appearances, and nothing can establish the finite between these two infinities that surround it and flee from it.

*   *   *

If a man begins by examining himself, he will see how it is impossible for him to transcend the finite. How can a part possibly know the whole? But perhaps he hopes at least to know the parts which are of the same dimensions as himself? The parts of the world have such a connection and interrelationship that I believe it is impossible to know one without the other or without the whole.

Man, for example, has a connection with all that he knows. He needs space to occupy and time to endure, movement to live, elements to form his body, warmth, nourishment from foods, and air to breathe. He sees the light, he feels bodies; in a word, everything has some relationship to him. Hence it follows that to understand man, one must know why he needs air to live; and to understand air, one must know how it has this connection with the life of man, etc.

A flame cannot exist without air; thus to know one it is necessary to know the other.

Thus everything being both a cause and an effect, dependent and supporting, mediate and immediate, and being connected by a natural and imperceptible bond which links the most remote and the most different things, I hold it to be impossible to know the parts without knowing the whole, and equally so to know the whole without knowing each of its particular parts. . .

Finally to complete the proof of our weakness I shall finish by these two considerations. . .

200. Man is but a reed, the weakest thing in nature; but it is a thinking reed. It is not necessary that the entire universe take up

arms to crush him; a breath, a drop of water suffices to kill him. But when the universe does crush him, man will still be nobler than that which kills him, since he knows that he dies; he knows the advantage the universe has over him. The universe knows nothing of this.

All our dignity thus consists in thought. It is here that we ought to elevate ourselves, and not in space and time, which we cannot fill. Thus let us labor to think well; this is the principle of morality.

201. The eternal silence of these infinite spaces frightens me.

228. What do the prophets say of Jesus Christ? That he will obviously be God? No, but that he is truly a hidden God, that he will be misunderstood, that we will not know who he is, that he will be a stumbling-block on which many shall fall, etc.

Thus let no one reproach us with lack of clarity, since it is that which we profess. . . .

232. We can understand nothing of the works of God if we do not take it as an axiom that he has willed to blind some and to enlighten others.

236. To blind. To enlighten. St. Aug[ustine] Monta[i]g[ne] Sebonde. There is enough clarity to enlighten the elect and enough obscurity to humble them. There is enough obscurity to blind the reprobate and enough clarity to condemn them and render them without excuse. . . .

If God had allowed only one religion it would have been too obvious. But let us look more closely; we shall discern the true one amidst this confusion. . . .

284. The only religion against nature, against common sense, against our pleasures, and the only one which has always existed.

418. [The Wager]

Infinity nothing.

Our soul is cast into the body where it finds number, time, and dimensions. On this it bases its reasoning, calls it nature and necessity, and cannot believe anything else.

One added to infinity does not increase it, any more than a foot extends an infinite length. In the presence of the infinite the finite disappears and becomes pure nothingness. Likewise our intellects before God; likewise our justice before the divine justice. There is not so great a disproportion between our justice and that of God as between one and infinity.

The justice of God must needs be as enormous as his mercy. And his justice toward the reprobate is less enormous, and should be less shocking, than his mercy toward the elect.

We know that there is an infinite, yet are ignorant of its nature; we know only that it is false that all numbers are finite. Hence it is true that there is an infinite number, but we do not know what it is. It is not odd, nor is it even, since adding one to it does not change its nature. Yet it is a number; and all numbers are either odd or even (this certainly holds for all finite numbers).

In the same way we can know that there is a God without knowing what he is. Is there no one substantial truth, seeing there are so many true things which are nevertheless not truth itself?

We know of the existence and nature of the finite since we too are finite and spatially extended. We know of the existence of the infinite but are ignorant of its nature, because it is extended as we are but, unlike us, is without any limits. But we know neither the existence nor the nature of God, because he has neither extension nor limit. Yet by faith we know of his existence and in glory we shall know his nature.

Now I have already shown that one can know of the existence of a thing without knowing its nature.

Let us speak now according to the light of nature.

If there is a God he is infinitely beyond comprehension, since, having neither parts nor limits, he can have no relationship with us. We are thus incapable of knowing what he is, or if he is. This being so, who will dare attempt to resolve this question? It cannot be we who have no relationship at all to him.

Who will thus blame the Christians for not being able to provide a rational justification for their belief, since they profess a religion for which they cannot give such a justification? In manifesting it before the world they declare that it is folly (*stultitia*)—and then you complain because they do not prove it! If they prove it they will betray it. It is in lacking proof that they prove themselves not lacking in sense.

"Yes, but although this excuses those who have offered such a proof, and takes away any blame for having produced it without reason, it does not excuse those who have accepted it."

"Let us examine this point. We say God exists, or he does not exist. But to which side shall we incline? Reason can do nothing to decide the question; an infinite chaos separates us, and at the other

end of that infinite distance a game is being played: heads or tails?*
How should we call it? Following reason you cannot do either; and
following reason you cannot leave either undone. Do not condemn
the falseness of those who have made their choice, for you know
nothing about it."

"No, but I condemn them not for having made this particular
choice, but for having chosen at all; for they who call it heads or
tails are equally wrong; the right thing is not to bet."

"'Yes, but you must bet. There is no choice; you are embarked.
Now which will you take? Let's see; since you must choose, which
concerns you least? You have two things to lose: the true and the
good; and two things to stake: your reason and your will, your
knowledge and your happiness; and your nature has two things to
avoid: error and misery. Since you must choose, your reason is no
further offended by having to choose one rather than the other. So
that point is settled. But what about your happiness? Let us weigh
the gain and the loss in calling heads: that is, that God exists. Let
us calculate for the two cases: if you win, you win everything, and if
you lose, you lose nothing—don't wait, then. Bet!"

"This is admirable. Yet, I must bet, but perhaps I shall stake too
much."

"Let's see; since the chances to win and to lose are equal, if you
could only win two lives for one you might still wager. But what if
there were three lives to win? You would have to play (by necessity)
and when you are forced to play, it would be foolish not to bet your
life to win three lives, when the odds on winning and losing are
equal. But here there is an eternity of life and happiness. And since
it is true that even if there were an infinite number of chances, of
which only one would win for you, you would still be right in bet-
ting one to win two, and you would be stupid if, being forced to bet,
you refused to bet one life against three (even in a game where there
was only one winning chance out of an infinite number) if there were
an infinity of infinitely happy life to win. But here there is an infinity of infinitely happy life to win and one chance of winning
against a finite number of chances of losing; and your stake is finite.
That clinches it; where the gain is infinite and the odds against
winning are finite, there is no point in calculating further—we
must bet everything. . . ."

"I confess it, I acknowledge it—but still, is there no means to see
the faces of the cards?"

* *Croix ou pile:* the obverse of the French coins of the time was marked with a
cross, which adds to the power of Pascal's imagery of wagering on Christianity.

"Yes, the Scriptures and the rest, etc."

"Yes, but I am bound and gagged; I am forced to bet; I am not at liberty; I am not released and I am so made that I cannot believe. What then do you want to do?"

"That is true; but at least you can realize that your inability to believe arises from your passions. Since your reason leads you to it but nevertheless you balk, labor to diminish your passions, not to convince yourself by multiplying the proofs of God. You wish to reach faith, but you do not know the path. You wish to cure yourself of unbelief and you ask the remedies for it; learn from those who have been bound like you and who now wager all their goods. These are men who know the path that you would follow and who have been cured of the disease of which you wish to be cured—so follow the way by which they began. This was by doing everything as if they believed: taking holy water, hearing masses, etc. By nature even that will make you believe and will make you stupid.*

"But it is that which I fear."

"Why? What have you to lose? But to show you that this leads you where you want to go, that this lessens the passions which are your great obstacles, etc.,

THE END OF THIS DISCOURSE:

"Now what evil can come to you in taking this decision? You will be faithful, honest, humble, grateful, charitable, friendly, sincere, true. . . . In truth you will be free of those foul pleasures, glory and luxury, but will you not have other things?

"I tell you that you will win in this life, and that with each step that you take along this path you will see so much certainty of gain, and so much of the nothingness of that which you risk, that you will know at the end that you have bet on an infinite sure thing for which you have given nothing at all."

"O this discourse enraptures me, transports me, etc."

"If this discourse pleases you and seems cogent to you, know that it is made by a man who before and afterwards has been on his knees praying to this infinite being without parts to whom he submits all that he has, for you to yield to him also all that is yours, for your own good and for his glory; so that strength may come to the help of weakness."

---

* *Vous abêtira*: the French allows the meaning "make you like a beast (*bête*)"; and since Pascal begins the sentence with *naturellement,* it is appropriate in interpreting this famous and difficult passage to consider what he has said about custom and nature: cf. *Pensées* 125 and 126, above p. 154.

423. The heart has its reasons which the reason does not know; one sees this in a thousand things.

I say that the heart naturally loves the universal being and naturally loves the self, according to how it gives itself up to one or the other. And it hardens itself against one or the other at will. You have rejected one and cherished the other—is it by reason that you love yourself?

424. It is the heart that feels God and not the reason. This is what faith is: God felt by the heart, not by the reason.

449. The God of Christians is not a God who is merely the author of the axioms of geometry and the order of the elements; that is the lot of the pagans and Epicureans. He is not only a God who exerts his providence over the life and goods of men, in order to give a happy life to those who worship him; that is the heritage of the Jews. But the God of Abraham, the God of Isaac, the God of Jacob, the God of Christians, is a God of love and of consolation. He is a God who fills the heart and soul of those whom he possesses; he is a God who makes them feel in their inward parts their misery and his infinite mercy; who makes his dwelling place in the depths of their souls; who fills them with humility, with joy, with confidence, with love; who makes it impossible for them to have any other end than himself.

All those who seek God outside of Jesus Christ and who remain content to search for him in nature either find no illumination which satisfies them or else it happens that they conceive a means of knowing God and serving him without a mediator, and through this fall either into atheism or into deism, two things which the Christian religion holds in almost equal abhorrence. . . .

562. There are only two kinds of men: the just who consider themselves sinners, and the sinners who consider themselves just.

678. Man is neither angel nor beast; and misfortune would have it that he who would play the angel plays the beast.

696. Let no one say that I have said nothing new; the arrangement of subjects is new. When we play tennis we both use the same ball, but one places it better. . . .

887. Descartes useless and uncertain.

905. Pyrrhonism.*

* A position of total skepticism or disbelief in everything, which took its name from the half-legendary Greek philosopher Pyrrho. Most contemporaries of Pascal would have thought of Montaigne (1533-1592) as the most famous modern Pyrrhonist.

In this world everything is true in part, false in part. Essential truth is not thus; it is entirely pure and true. This admixture of falsehood destroys it and brings it to nought. Nothing is purely true, and thus nothing is simply true from the standpoint of pure truth. We say that it is true that homicide is evil—yes, for we know well the evil and the false. But of what shall we say that it is good? Chastity? I say not, for the race would come to an end. Marriage? No, continence is better. Not to kill? No, for the consequent disorders would be horrible, and evil men would kill all the good. To kill? No, for that destroys nature. We have neither the true nor the good except in part, and mixed up with the evil and the false.

926. We make an idol of truth itself, for truth removed from charity is not God; it is a reflection of him and an idol which we must neither love nor worship. Still less must we love and admire its opposite, which is falsehood. . . .

1001. I cannot forgive Descartes; he would have preferred, in all of his philosophy, to do without God; but he could not help allowing him to give a flick of the finger to set the universe in motion. After that he has nothing further for God to do.

Pascal's "Memorial" *

The year of grace 1654.
Monday 23 November, the day of St. Clement, pope and martyr, and of other holy martyrs.
The eve of St. Chrysogone, martyr, and other saints.
From about half past ten until half past twelve at night.

Fire.

God of Abraham, God of Isaac, God of Jacob, not of the philosophers and scholars.
Certainty, certainty, feeling, joy, peace.
God of Jesus Christ
God of Jesus Christ.
My God and thy God. [John xx, 17]

* After Pascal's death a maid by chance discovered that a bulge in the lining of his doublet concealed a piece of parchment and one of paper. The way in which the pieces had been folded and refolded indicates that Pascal took care to sew them into the lining of each new garment he wore. On both the words above had been written in Pascal's hand.

Thy God shall be my God. [Ruth i, 16]
Forgetting the world and everything except God.
He can only be found by the ways taught in the Gospel.
Greatness of the human soul.
Just Father, the world has not known thee, but I have known thee.
[John xvii, 25]
Joy, joy, joy, tears of joy. . . .

A Chronological Table*

Year	Floruit	Died	Writings	Public Affairs
1600		BRUNO [c.48] HOOKER [53]	Coke, *Reports* (-16); Gilbert, *Magnetic Bodies*; Shakespeare, Hamlet; Twelfth Night	
1601	KEPLER [30]	BRAHE [46]	Charron, *Of Wisdom*	
1602	DONNE [31]		Campanella, City of the Sun (pub. 1643); Shakespeare, Troilus and Cressida	Dutch East India Company founded.
1603	JONSON [37]	GILBERT [44]	Althusius, *Politics*	Elizabeth I dies; James VI of Scotland becomes English king.
1604			Cervantes, *Don Quixote* I; Shakespeare, Othello	Anglo-Spanish war, begun in 1588, concluded
1605			Bacon, *Advancement of Learning*; Shakespeare, King Lear	Gunpowder Plot foiled. Death of Tsar Boris Godunov. Paul V elected Pope.
1606			Jonson, Volpone; Shakespeare, Macbeth	
1607	BURTON [40] RUBENS [40]	BARONIUS [38]	Shakespeare, Antony and Cleopatra	Jamestown colony founded.
1608	HARVEY [57]	LA POPELINIÈRE [40?]	Grotius, *Freedom of Seas*	

* "Floruit" means reached age of 30; superscript number is year of death. Superscript number in "Died" column is year of birth. Italic titles in "Writings" published this year; Roman titles first performance of plays or beginning of writing of subsequently published book.

1609	ARMINIUS[60]	Bacon: *Wisdom of the Ancients* / Kepler: *New Astronomy*	12-year truce between Spain & Dutch. Bank of Amsterdam founded. Moriscos expelled from Spain.
1610		Jonson: The Alchemist / Galileo: *The Sidereal Messenger*	Murder of Henri IV; Louis XIII king of France. Remonstrance of Dutch Arminians.
1611		"King James" Bible / Shakespeare: Winter's Tale; The Tempest	
1612	GROTIUS[45]	Góngora: The Solitudes	
1613	LORD HERBERT OF CHERBURY[48]	Galileo: *Letters on Sunspots*	Mikhail Romanov (founder of dynasty) becomes Tsar.
1614	SELDEN[54] / EL GRECO[41]	Cervantes: *Don Quixote II* / Napier: *Logarithms* / Selden: *Titles of Honor* / Webster: Duchess of Malfi	Last meeting of French Estates General before 1789.
1615	CERVANTES[4] / PASQUIER[29]		
1616	SHAKESPEARE[5-]	Chapman: *Homer* / James I: *Works*	
1617	SUÁREZ[48]		
1618	RALEGH[52?] / HOBBES[70]	Selden: *History of Tithes*	Beginning of 30 Years' War in Bohemian revolt.
1619		Kepler: *Harmony of the World* (announces 3rd law)	Dutch Calvinism triumphs at Synod of Dort; Ferdinand II H. R. Emperor; Elector Palatine elected King of Bohemia.

Year	Floruit	Died	Writings	Public Affairs
1620			Bacon: *New Organon*	Battle of the White Mountain; Hapsburg armies overrun Bohemia. Voyage of the Mayflower.
1621		BELLARMINE[42]	Burton: *Anatomy of Melancholy*	Bacon impeached; Coke, Selden, and others imprisoned for opposition to James I.
1622	GASSENDI[55]			
1623	GEORGE HERBERT[33]	CAMDEN[51]	Shakespeare: *First Folio* Galileo: *The Assayer*	Urban VIII elected Pope.
1624	POUSSIN[65]		Herbert of Cherbury: *Of Truth*	Richelieu chief minister of France (-42).
1625		JAMES I[65]	Bacon: *Essays* (3rd. ed.) Grotius: *Rights of War and Peace*	Charles I king of England. Anglo-Spanish war. Rebellion of Huguenots.
1626	DESCARTES[50]	BACON[61]		Huguenots besieged at La Rochelle; English expedition fails. Hapsburg generals defeat Protestants.
1627			Bacon: *New Atlantis*	Franco-Spanish war breaks out in Italy. Tilly & Wallenstein reach North Sea.

Year		Works	Events
1628	BERNINI[80]	Coke: *Institutes* I Descartes: Rules for the Direction of the Mind (pub. 1701) Harvey: *Motion of Heart and Blood*	La Rochelle surrenders. Charles I's favorite Buckingham assassinated; Petition of Right enacted.
1629	VAN DYCK[41] VELÁZQUEZ[60]	Hobbes translation of *Peloponnesian War*	Charles I's third parliament dissolved after stormy scenes; no further until 1640. Edict of Restitution in Germany.
1630	KEPLER[71] CALDERÓN[81] LORRAIN[82]		Anglo-French and Anglo-Spanish wars ended. "Great migration" to New England. Gustavus Adolphus lands in Pomerania.
1631	DONNE[72] FERMAT[65]	Milton: L'Allegro; Il Penseroso	Peace between France & Spain. Magdeburg sacked by Tilly's men; Swedes defeat Tilly at Leipzig.
1632		Galileo: *Dialogue on the Two Chief World-Systems*	Gustavus Adolphus killed after his armies conquered N. Germany; Christina Queen of Sweden.
1633	GEORGE HERBERT[93]	Donne: *Poems*	Galileo forced to abjure by Inquisition. Laud Archbishop of Canterbury; Strafford in Ireland.
1634	COKE[52]	Milton: Comus	Wallenstein murdered. First Ship Money levy.

CHRONOLOGICAL TABLE (continued)

Year	Floruit	Died	Writings	Public Affairs
1635	SIR THOMAS BROWNE[82]	LOPE DE VEGA[82]		French Academy founded under Richelieu's patronage; subsidies paid Hapsburg opponents. Ship Money held legal and extended.
1636	CORNEILLE[84] REMBRANDT[69]		Corneille: Le Cid	
1637		JONSON[78]	Descartes: Discourse on Method	Ferdinand II dies; Ferdinand III elected emperor.
1638	MILTON[74]	ALTHUSIUS[57]	Galileo: Two New Sciences Milton: Lycidas	Scottish Covenant taken to resist Anglican missal & canons.
1639	CLARENDON[74]	CAMPANELLA[68]	Corneille: Horace	First Bishops' War in Scotland.
1640		BURTON[77] RUBENS[77]	Donne: LXXX Sermons Jansenius: Augustinus	Second Bishops' War; Charles I, bankrupt, forced to call parliament, which impeaches Laud & Strafford. Portuguese and Catalonian revolts against Spain. Frederick William Elector of Brandenburg.
1641	HARRINGTON[77]	SPELMAN[61?] VAN DYCK[95]	Descartes: Meditations	Strafford executed; Long Parliament enacts many reforms. Grand Remonstrance.
1642	SAMUEL BUTLER[80]	GALILEO[64]	Coke: Institutes II Hobbes: De Cive	Fighting begins between royal and parliamentary armies.

1643	LA ROCHEFOUCAULD[80]	Arnauld: *Frequent Communion* Browne: *Religion of a Doctor* Corneille: *Polyeucte* Milton: *Doctrine of Divorce*	Louis XIII dies; Louis XIV (age 5) king; Anne of Austria Regent, Mazarin chief minister, etc. French defeat Spanish at Rocroi. Episcopacy abolished in England.
1644	HENRY MORE[87]	Descartes: *Principles of Philosophy*	First decisive parliamentary victory at Marston Moor.
1645	BAXTER[91] LILBURNE[57]	Coke: *Institutes III & IV* Milton: *Areopagitica: Of Education* Lilburne: *England's Birthright Justified*	New Model Army formed; royalists routed at Naseby.
1646		Browne: *Plague of Fallacies* Clarendon: History of the Rebellion (-71; pub. 1704)	First Civil War ends; Charles I takes refuge with Scots; C. of E. made Presbyterian.
1647	LORD HERBERT OF CHERBURY[83]		Naples revolts against Spain. William II Dutch stadholder.
1648			Peace of Westphalia ends 30 Years' War. First Fronde. Second English Civil War.
1649	LE BRUN[90]	Descartes: *Passions of the Soul*	Charles I executed; monarchy and Lords abolished. Second Fronde.
1650	DESCARTES[96]	Hobbes: *Human Nature*	Cromwell routs Scottish armies supporting Charles II.
1651	LA FONTAINE[95] MARVELL[78]	Hobbes: *Leviathan*	English parliament passes Navigation Acts.

Year	Floruit	Died	Writings	Public Affairs
1652	MOLIÈRE[73]			Anglo-Dutch War. Irish rebellion stamped out. Barcelona surrenders to Spanish army.
1653	PASCAL[62] PETTY[87]	FILMER	Walton: *Compleat Angler*	Both Frondes crushed. Jan de Witt pensionary of Holland. Cromwell named Lord Protector.
1654	FOX[92]	SELDEN[84]		Peace between Dutch and English. Christina of Sweden abdicates.
1655		GASSENDI[92]		Anglo-Spanish war.
1656	de SÉVIGNÉ[96]		Harrington: *Oceana* Pascal: *Provincial Letters*	Readmission of Jews to England.
1657	BOSSUET[04] BOYLE[91]	HARVEY[78] LILBURNE[16?]		Dutch and Portuguese go to war over Brazil.
1658	BUNYAN[88]		Browne: *Urn Burial*	Oliver Cromwell dies; Richard Cromwell Protector. French crush Spanish army (Battle of the Dunes).
1659	CHRISTIAAN HUYGENS[95]		More: *Immortality of the Soul*	Peace of the Pyrenees ends Franco-Spanish war. Louis XIV marries Spanish Infanta. End of the Protectorate.

1660	VELÁZQUEZ[90]	Boyle: *Weight and Spring of the Air* Pepys: *Diary* (-69; pub. 1825)	Long Parliament dissolved. Restoration of Charles II. Royal Society founded.
1661	DRYDEN[00]	Boyle: *Sceptical Chemist* Glanville: *Vanity of Dogmatizing*	Death of Mazarin; Louis XIV to rule henceforth in his own person. First act of parliament against Dissenters.
1662	PASCAL[23] LOCKE[04] MABILLON[07] PUFENDORF[94] SPINOZA[77] VERMEER[75] WREN[23]	Arnaulds: *Port Royal Logic* Descartes: *On Man* Molière: School for Wives	Colbert controller-general of finances (-83).
1663	PEPYS[03]	Butler: Hudibras (-78)	
1664			**British seize New Amsterdam.**
1665	POUSSIN[94] FERMAT[01]	Hooke: *Micrographia* Molière: Dom Juan La Rochefoucauld: *Maxims*	Second Anglo-Dutch war begins. Plague in London. Charles II (the Sufferer) King of Spain.
1666	BOILEAU[11]	Bunyan: *Grace Abounding* Molière: Misanthrope	Louvois minister of war (-91). French Academy of Sciences founded. Great Fire of London.
1667		Milton: *Paradise Lost* More: *Divine Dialogues; Handbook of Ethics* Molière: Tartuffe Racine: Andromaque Sprat: *History of Royal Society*	France, England, Netherlands, and Denmark sign Treaty of Breda. Lord Chancellor Clarendon impeached.

Year	Floruit	Died	Writings	Public Affairs
1668	MALEBRANCHE[15] SIMON[12]		Dryden: *Of Dramatic Poesy* Molière: The Miser	Independence of Portugal recognized by Spain.
1669	RACINE[99]	REMBRANDT[06]	Racine: Britannicus Aubrey: Brief Lives (-96; pub. 1813)	
1670			Pascal: *Pensées* Spinoza: *Theological-Political Treatise*	Secret Treaty of Dover between France and England.
1671			Locke: Essay on Human Understanding (-90) Milton: *Paradise Regained; Samson Agonistes*	
1672	NEWTON[27]		Molière: Learned Ladies Newton: Optics (pub. 1704) Pufendorf: *On the Law of Nature and Nations*	France & England attack Dutch; French overrun most of country; Jan de Witt murdered by mob; William III becomes Stadholder.
1673		MOLIÈRE[22]	Molière: Imaginary Invalid Pufendorf: *Duty of Man and Citizen*	
1674	PENN[18]	CLARENDON[09] MILTON[08]	Boileau: *Art of Poetry*	Peace between Dutch & English. Empire joins war against France.
1675		VERMEER[32]	Bunyan: *Pilgrim's Progress*	
1676	LEIBNIZ[16]		Etherege: Man of Mode	Innocent XI elected Pope.

Year			Works	Events
1677	BAYLE[06]	HARRINGTON[11] SPINOZA[32]	Racine: *Phèdre* Spinoza: *Ethics*	
1678		MARVELL[21]	Cudworth: *Intellectual System of the Universe* Huygens: *Treatise on Light* (pub. 1690) Simon: *Critical History of the Old Testament*	Treaties of Nimwegen (-79). General European peace. "Popish Plot" in England.
1679		HOBBES[88]	Locke: *Two Treatises of Government* (-81) Filmer: *Freeholder's Grand Inquest*	Whigs attempt to exclude Duke of York (future James II) from the succession. Habeas Corpus Act; Rebellion of Scottish Covenanters.
1680		BERNINI[98] BUTLER[12] LA ROCHEFOUCAULD[13]		
1681	FÉNELON[15]	CALDERÓN[00]	Bossuet: *Universal History* Dryden: *Absalom & Achitophel* Mabillon: *On Diplomatic*	Charles II calls and immediately dissolves fifth parliament. France annexes Strasbourg.
1682		BROWNE[05] LORRAIN[00]	Dryden: *Religio Laici* Hobbes: *Behemoth*	
1683			Bayle: *Comet of 1680* Burnet: *History of My Own Time* (-04: pub. 1724) Fontenelle: *Dialogues of the Dead*	France invades Austrian Netherlands. Charles II revokes charters of English towns; Russell & Sidney executed; Locke & Shaftesbury flee to Holland.

CHRONOLOGICAL TABLE (continued)

Year	Floruit	Died	Writings	Public Affairs
1684		CORNEILLE[06]	Brady: *Old English History* Malebranche: *Treatise on Morals*	"Dragonnades" and other efforts at forcible conversion of Huguenots.
1685			Halifax: Character of a Trimmer	Revocation of Edict of Nantes. Charles II dies; James II king of England. Monmouth's rebellion; "Bloody Assizes."
1686			Fontenelle: *On the Plurality of Worlds*	
1687	FONTENELLE[57]	HENRY MORE[14] PETTY[23]	Dryden: *Hind and Panther* Fénélon: *Education of Girls* Fontenelle: *History of Oracles* Newton: *Mathematical Principles of Natural Philosophy*	James II issues Declaration of Liberty of Conscience.
1688		BUNYAN[28]	Bossuet: *Variations in Protestantism* Fontenelle: *Digression on Ancients and Moderns*	Seven Bishops acquitted on seditious libel. William III invited to England; lands and James II flees.
1689	PURCELL[95]		Locke: *Letter concerning Toleration* Racine: *Esther* Simon: *Critical History of Text of New Testament*	William III and Mary made rulers of England; Bill of Rights and Toleration Act. England joins alliance against Louis XIV.

1690	DEFOE[31]	LE BRUN[19]	Locke: *Essay concerning Human Understanding*; *Two Treatises of Government* / Racine: Athalie	William III defeats James II at Battle of the Boyne. War of the League of Augsburg begins.
1691				
1692	BENTLEY[42]	BAXTER[15]		
1693		BOYLE[27]	Locke: *Thoughts on Education*	Beginning of English national debt.
1694		PUFENDORF[32]		Bank of England founded. Licensing Act not renewed.
1695		LA FONTAINE[21] CHRISTIAAN HUYGENS[29] PURCELL[59]	Locke: *Reasonableness of Christianity*	
1696		DE SÉVIGNÉ[26]	Toland: *Christianity Not Mysterious*	
1697		SWIFT[45]	Bayle: *Historical and Critical Dictionary* / Swift: Battle of the Books (pub. 1704)	Treaty of Ryswick between France, England, Spain, and Holland; France and Empire also make peace.
1698	VICO[44]			London Stock Exchange founded.
1699		RACINE[30]	Fénelon: *Telemachus*	
1700	CONGREVE[29] MANDEVILLE[33]	DRYDEN[31]	Congreve: Way of the World / Fénelon: *Dialogues of the Dead*	Charles II of Spain dies; Louis XIV proclaims his grandson king of Spain. Berlin Academy founded.